TO OUR READERS

Hail guest! We ask not what thou art;
If friend, we greet thee hand & heart;
If stranger, no longer be;
If foe, our love shall conquer thee.

Traditional Welsh Welcome Blessing

DIF. FE. REN. CES

This book is a loving donation
to the work of our friends in

GREENPEACE

1611 Connecticut Ave., N.W.
Washington, D.C. 20009
[(202) 462-1177]

* & *

430 W. Erie St.
Chicago, Illinois 60610
[(312) 440-1860]

❖ DEDICATION ❖

For Sadako Sasaki &
all the children
in the world,
no matter how lifeclothed:
whether in flesh
fur, feathers, fins
shells or leaves
in all their diversity...
May all living beings be happy!

Grateful acknowledgment is made to the following people for permission to reprint copyrighted material: All work by Peggy Lipschutz; "Virgule", Philippe Collot; "My Rainbow Race", Pete Seeger, (NY, NY, Sanga Music, '70/'72); "It's a Good Thing I'm Not in Charge Here" and "Life is a Cosmic Bivouac", Evi Seidman, '87; "The Adventures of a Little Sparrow", Yukari Kadoguchi, (Fukuoka, Japan, Araki Shoten, '56/'57); The Diary of Anne Frank, (London, Vallentine, Mitchell, & Co., Ltd.); "Seed Corn Must Not Be Ground", Käthe Kollwitz, (NY, NY, Galerie St. Etienne); "Hibakusha: Mrs. Motoyo Fujiwara", Ittetsu Morishita; "Pearl Nakkai", Geoff Manasse; "Warnings" and "Family Promise", Holly Near, (Oakland, CA, Hereford Music, '79 and '82), "Dancing on the silos..." and "30,000 women...", Raissa Page, (London, Format, '83 and '82), "Mother and Child", Käthe Kollwitz, (West Berlin, Galerie Pels-Leusden); "The Poor Elephants of the Ueno Zoo", Kobe City University of Foreign Studies, Student Body Association, and Zenshin-Za Theater Company for Children, Japan; "The Little Fishes and Chiko in the Sea", Ryozo Yagi and RNC Theater Company, (Takamatsu, Japan); "Song for a Russian Mother", Holly Gwinn Graham, (LaConner, WA, Harbor Seal Publishing, '82); "We Shall Bring Forth New Life", Sadako Kurihara; "The White Ship on the Dream Island", Akio Araki and Kyogei Puppet Theater, (Kyoto, Japan); "Fighting Leads to Losses", Cathy Spagnoli; "We Hate to See Them Go", Malvina Reynolds, (Berkeley, CA, Schroder Music Co., '59); "War Preparers Anonymous", Kurt Vonnegut, (NY, NY, The Nation: 7 January, '84); "The Monster of St.Lawrence Island", Grace Cross Antoghame Akumelingekuk; "The Earth is Our Mother". Karl Jadrnicek; "The Dove and the Hawk", Fritz Eichenberg, (Chicago, IL, The Peace Museum); "Tickling the Baby", Nina Uccello; and "Affirmation", Nancy Schimmel. All rights reserved. Written permission required from any of the above to use their material, but feel free to tell the stories on in your own words.

© 1987 by Floating Eaglefeather,
 ...And the Earth Lived Happily Ever After...

ISBN 0-9618778-0-4

Printed in New Orleans, LA.

Published by: Wages of Peace
                       309 Trudeau Drive
                       Metairie, LA 70003

...And the Earth Lived

happily ever after...

Old and New Traditional Tales to Wage Peace

Edited by: Floating Eaglefeather
- storyteller -

Foreword by: Ernest Sternglass
- radiation physicist -

Graphic Artist: Peggy Lipschutz

Calligrapher: Rebecca Armstrong

Wages of Peace

FOREWORD

It was on Hiroshima Day, August 5, 1983, in Washington, D.C. that I first met Eaglefeather. I had come to the small church near the Capitol where the conferences took place in which I discussed the world-wide effects of nuclear bomb-fallout on the newborn. Eaglefeather had been asked to tell stories to the children that would teach them about the atomic bomb, and how all of us working together will make sure that such a terrible weapon would never be used again.

In the evening over dinner, we talked of our common concern for the children everywhere, who would never have a chance to live their lives if nuclear war were to break out. We agreed that only by reaching the people all over the globe with the story of the real implications of such a war, and what it would do to all living things could we hope to halt the drift towards holocaust that governments appear unwilling or unable to stop. Yet, despite the mounting evidence that it is the children who will be most strongly affected by the world-wide fallout, and perhaps because of this, I have a strong feeling of hope. For if both young and old people all over the world could learn of the truly suicidal nature of nuclear weapons for the entire human species, they would find ways to persuade government leaders to dismantle the bombs, ending forever the threat hanging over all the children in our world ever since Hiroshima and Nagasaki.

In this hope, I was greatly encouraged by a story Eaglefeather told me about something that had happened just a few hours before our dinner. A bit earlier in the day, he had taught the children in his group how to fold paper cranes, in memory of Sadako Sasaki. The plan was to take the children to the steps of the Capitol to give the cranes to passers-by. The conference organizer, Louise Franklin-Ramirez, had called the police, and had been told that no permit would be needed for a small group of children, and so they started out hopefully on their mission for peace.

When they got to the park surrounding the Capitol, they were stopped by two police officers who told them that without a permit to demonstrate, they would have to go back. In consternation, they turned to each other, trying to think what to do. Not wanting to go back without having given away their paper cranes, they would hand out the cranes to passers-by, while walking back to the church, and explain what they signified.

When they had gotten almost half-way back to the church, a young man, who had apparently been running after them, caught up with the children, and asked whether he could interview them for the Cable News. He had seen from a distance what had happened, and had decided it would make a good story for the evening news. So the children told to the best of their ability why they had made the cranes, and why they were handing them to the people passing.

So, despite the attempt of the bureaucracy to prevent the children from making their plea for peace to a few visitors to the Capitol steps, the very attempt to deny them this opportunity gave them a chance to be heard by millions, adding to the swelling demand for an end to the madness that ultimately no government in the world will be able to resist.

Because the universe is beautiful, it is worth saving for the children, and worth saving the children for the universe.

27 January 1985
Bloomington, Indiana

Ernest J. Sternglass, Ph. D.

Ernest J Sternglass

INTRODUCTION

"This book is not a solitary lament or an emanation from darkness, but rather a direct and aimed weapon...Poetry has always had the purity of water or of fire which cleans or burns without doubt. (...) I swear...that my poetry will serve and sing of dignity to the indignant, of hope to the hopeless, of justice in spite of the unjust, of equality in spite of exploiters, of truth in spite of liars." The power of poetry for Neruda is the same power a storyteller feels for story, a radiation physicist for a felt discovery, a graphic artist for an image of beauty as truth, or a calligrapher for a relaxed disciplined line. The four of us work together for the power of peace as we see it in a child's play, aiming our love to transmute words into action, bombs into bridges. We hope this book will give adults stories to tell their children to better enable them to understand our world's need for peace--and will also give adults the impetus to work for a world with better conditions for all children.

Many people consider peace a condition that simply occurs when there is no war. However, many people think peace is a very definite activity into which equal or greater energy must be given than the waging of war because war is less challenging than peace. To those of us who think and feel this way, the challenge of working with children and sharing their smiles, questions, and needs is greater than the challenge to create machines that will kill any of them anywhere in the world. This concept grows in an organic manner as we learn more and more about the struggles our neighbors are undergoing in other parts of the world, and see so much energy being given to military preparations which are presumably never going to be used because they are being built(!). We build a road to Peace as we kill the small ideas of separatism within each of us that keep us chained to an unbalanced materialism, and threaten all of us with death. At each moment, we seek ways to help this world's lives have a chance to continue in healthy happiness.

Mahatma Gandhi's advice to the satyagrahis -- followers of the force of truth -- when they were heading towards a potential site for civil disobedience against immoral laws was that they fast, to abstain from food would make them more vulnerable, and more able to see and to expose the untruth in the law to transform it to truth. Ernest Sternglass' work has been in discovering how the most vulnerable members of our society -- the unborn, the newborn, the children, and the very elderly -- suffer from low-level radiation. Based on U.S.A. Monthly Vital Statistics Report, 1983 Summary, he has discovered that the U.S. crude and age-adjusted death rates declined from 1930 until 1954, then leveled out and rose slightly to a peak in 1968, then declined sharply from 1968-75. This decline, submits Dr. Sternglass, is due to a few years of no atmospheric atomic bomb tests and few nuclear reactors. Adding three to five years for the delayed effect that heart disease and leukemia show when reactors started to proliferate and atomic bomb tests continued, and the curved place between the curved line as it would have continued if death rates had continued declining as they had from 1930-1954, and the way it changed following the atomic tests and power plants, gives nine million deaths above normal expectations. This is in the U.S.A. alone -- about ten times this number have died in the world. These are subtle deaths, not violent like a bomb or a gun, and are the casualties of the cold war. These children, unborn and stillborn, have been the satyagrahis whose vulnerability has put them into suffering and death to expose immoral laws and to help us to find ways to transform these to truth.

A scientific study is based upon observation of repeated physical phenomena. A traditional story is formed upon intuitive observation of repeated emotional phenomena, and deserves equal recognition to the scientific studies. As the interpretations of poems and stories changes over the years, they can now warn us of the doom into which we hurl ourselves if we continue to allow the power of the sun to harness us. The stories show us ways that people in the past and in the present have found ways to challenge war with peace, and why we have to do it. These stories are important for us to know and to share because the war-lovers want to keep knowledge from people. We must all become storytellers, sharers of knowledge, our greatest tool to defeat war. These stories and ideas are only a few of those from which we can learn. We must especially seek out the visions and tales of yellow, red, and brown people, women, underprivileged, young, and old people. World politics has been reflecting values of white, male privilege, and we must make a conscious effort to give equal or greater power to the values of those who fall outside of this privileged position if we are to weave shut the rents and tears in our social fabric that make the building and dropping of atomic bombs -- or any kind of bombs -- and the building of atomic power plants a possibility. If we do this, privilege will become universal as everyone receives respect and love, food and drink, warmth and shelter, medical help and creative growth.

The hibakusha, those who have lived through the first atomic bombs dropped by human beings on other human beings, remind us that those who have lived through it feel no one could possibly do such a thing again, but that those who would push the button would not think as they do and would do it in the same way most of us do our day-to-day jobs. They were told by their government -- influenced by the U.S.A. military -- to accept their suffering quietly, for the good of the Japanese nation. There are now 370,000 hibakusha registered in Japan, with 70 of them dying each year since 1945 in the Hiroshima Hibakusha Hospital, where treatment and medicine are still unsatisfactory for radiation disease. They tell us that they will not be able to live life happily until we can assure them that their suffering has not been for nothing -- that we have become wiser through their suffering, and will create peace, so that no one else will have to live through what they continue to live each day. Ittetsu Morishita, who took the pictures of the "Hibakusha" section, said that he hoped that people would get a feeling of warmth for one hibakusha, and, feeling compassion for her suffering, from his pictures of her, would work to make sure no one else has a life story with as much tragedy as has been Mrs. Fujiwara's lot since August 6, 1945. We must think of these elderly victims of the bomb as our grandparents, from whom we learn as we sit at their feet. Gerry Armstrong, a storyteller, tells us that each one of us "has a thousand grandmothers. One is Jewish and one gentile. One black; one white. One Filipino, one Chinese. One eagle; one coyote. All the divided tribes of humanity are united in our humanity. We must honor all of our grandmothers with equal respect and joy." To this, I would add the paraphrase that each one of us has a thousand grandchildren, and they are the children of all the peoples of the world. The grandparents' love for their grandchildren must become our love for all children. The hibakusha grandparents tell us they want the children to live as long, and happier, than they have.

The Dogai Fukuryu Maru ("Fifth Lucky Dragon") is a notable personality in the world peace movement. For nine years, the Japanese hibakusha had remained silent at the behest of occupational forces from the U.S.A., and later from shame, but then the USA military detonated an H-bomb test in the Pacific Ocean, against the advice of scientists who warned them that the radioactive fallout would fall on inhabited islands. The Fukuryu Maru, forty miles away from the testing site, had a rain of radioactive ash that caused the death of its radio operator, Aikichi Kuboyama, in September of the same year, 1954. The Japanese people suddenly realized that the USA was not only not arresting its development of this awful bomb, but was making it uglier and bigger. Through the puppet play about the Fukuryu Maru, the child is gently introduced to a reality in the world about which they must learn if they are to live on this planet.

Our world home is now afire with nuclear preparations going on at the rate of one Hiroshima-bomb value of destructiveness every thirty minutes since the end of World War II. Meanwhile, children starve and go cold and are born with the diseases that a nuclear power plant presence in the neighborhood increases. We are all Herods and Pharaohs and Kamsas killing holy innocents unless we are working to create peace for all, happiness for all living beings.

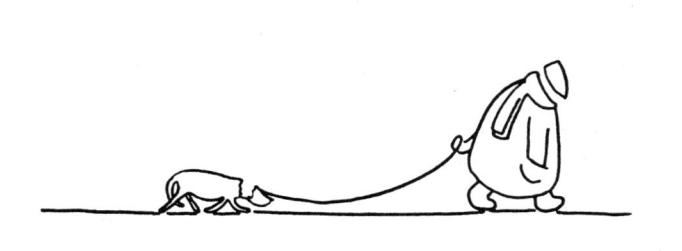

Even the injustice to animals and plants that atomic havoc wreaks is touched upon here. The fables are lighter, more humorous reminders of what humanity faces in every war: losses (always), and suffering (mostly to the poor, the very young, and the very old.) The last two stories are chosen for their psychological and spiritual strengths which a child can use in the creating of a society of peace. We wage peace for the children, and they teach us the fearlessness which we need in order to do this for them. We cannot trust the military leaders to tap into their own love of children, for they have been known to hide the negative effects of their testing and not release health studies linking leukemia and thyroid abnormalities to U.S.A. bomb test fallout (Dr. Caldicott calls plutonium "thalidomide forever") since it would "pose potential problems: adverse public reaction, lawsuits, and jeopardizing the programs at the Nevada Test Site." (The Washington Post, April, 1979.)

All profits from the sale of this book go to two organizations that are actively waging peace for all living beings in very different, inspired, and inspiring ways: Greenpeace, and The Peace Museum. Greenpeace is a world-organization acting for peace directly, personally, and non-violently. These people put themselves between exploiters and animals, trees, or other people who would be exposed to sickness or death needlessly. Small boats in front of large whalers, their vulnerability is the peaceful tool with which they wage peace. The Peace Museum in Chicago is a changing array of exhibits dedicated to peace. Touring exhibits such as The Unforgettable Fire, images drawn by hibakusha, survivors of Hiroshima and Nagasaki; and The Ribbon: A Celebration of Life, segments from the 18-mile ribbon of things people wouldn't want to lose in a nuclear war; complement fixed exhibits such as Carrying Greenham Home: Greenham Common and Other Women's Peace Camps. Issues of war and peace are explored through visual, literary, and performing arts. (Note Beneficial: Peggy, Rebecca, and I met through The Peace Museum, so this book is also a loving labor of gratitude for having introduced three of us to a powerful friendship.) We hope you will find other opportunities to support these people in our work to create happiness for all life, together directly or indirectly.

Thanks are due for helping this book come into being to Ernest, Peggy, & Rebecca, first of all. Carol Partington's and Phillip Weinberger's support have also proved priceless. Philippe Collot is to be thanked for "Virgule", the peaceful person with the little dog who brighten the margins of these pages. To all of the contributors of the stories, poems, and photographs, much appreciation. And to you, the reader, for finding ways to communicate and to interrelate with young people (and all society!) to help allay their fears in a society that values peace verbally, but which fails to prove its commitment to harmony through its actions -- to your actions. Please tell the stories on in your own words...

When informed of our work on this book, the Information Department of the Soviet Women's Committee wrote to say that, "Waging peace deserves the closest attention as there is nothing more important today than to join efforts of all who cherish the ideal of peace and cooperation among people." Even though we may want to plunge into these efforts, when we learn of the terrors that are war and hunger, its twin, it may be hard not to feel paralysed. How can we accept this reality so we can work to change it? How can we help the children accept this reality so they can help us work to change it? The path from terror to action begins, in Dr. Helen Caldicott's words, when people "start feeling grief for their planet and their family; they have to enter a state of shock and disbelief, followed by depression and then anger, to swim the river of emotion which will enable them to decide what to do. I don't want them to avoid the discomfort or the pain. If they avoided it, they wouldn't be as effective. (...) To cure the planet, we must get rid of nuclear weapons. Period! (...) We can change, and we will!"

What, then, is the best way to plunge onto this road leading away from those twins, war and hunger, and towards harmony? Niki Koutsogiorga wipes away our doubts by telling us that, "Peace and Freedom are twins -- their mother is Fearlessness!"

So the only way we can create "...and the Earth lived happily ever after ..." is ... fearlessly!

River of Time
Earth, Universe, Heart of Spirit

Floating Eaglefeather

TABLE of CONTENTS

...And the Earth Lived Happily Ever After...--Peggy Lipschutz -- Cover
Welsh Welcome Blessing/Dedication/Cover Calligraphy -- Rebecca Armstrong
Foreword -- Ernest Sternglass, Ph.D.
Introduction -- Floating Eaglefeather
"Virgule" -- Philippe Collot -- Margins throughout book
My Rainbow Race * Pete Seeger * 13
"My Rainbow Race" * Peggy Lipschutz * 14
It's a Good Thing I'm Not in Charge Here * Evi Seidman * 15
The Story of Sadako Sasaki * 16
Sparrow's Adventures * Yukari Kadoguchi * 17
The Diary of Anne Frank * 3 May/15 July, '44 * 20
Seed Corn Must Not Be Ground * Käthe Kollwitz * 21
Picasso's Gift to the Peace Movement * 23
The Quaker's Stroke * Traditional * 23
The White Crane Woman * Bhavanii * 24
Hibakusha: Mrs. Motoyo Fujiwara * Ittetsu Morishita * 26
Sun Myth * a Kathlamet tale * 41
Pearl Nakkai * Geoff Manasse * 43
Warnings * Holly Near * 44
Fearlessness * Ananda Marga Monk (unidentified) * 45
The Seventh Sister * Women of Greenham Common * 46
Dancing on the Silos/30,000 Women * Raissa Page * 47/49
The Meditation Teacher and the Warrior * Tan Ratanando * 50
North East Germany, 1945 * Ursula Friedrichson * 51
Mother and Child * Käthe Kollwitz * 51
The Samurai and the Monk * Reuven Gold * 52
The Poor Elephants of the Ueno Zoo * KCUFS/SBA//Zenshin-Za Theater * 52
The Little Fishes and Chiko in the Sea * Ryozo Yagi * 55
He Pule * Pilahi Paki * 56
Song for a Russian Mother * Holly Gwinn Graham * 57
Traditional Paper Cut-out * Poland * 57
We Shall Bring Forth New Life * Sadako Kurihara * 58
Family Promise * Holly Near * 59
I Come and Stand * Nazim Hikmet * 60
Okori Jizo * Yuko Yamaguchi * 61
The White Ship on the Dream Island * Akio Araki * 61
Fighting Leads to Losses * Cathy Spagnoli * 63
The Frogs and the Bulls * Aesop * 63
The Snipe and the Mussel * Peng Tong * 64
Alexander and the Pirates * Gesta Romanorum * 64
Life is a Cosmic Bivouac * Evi Seidman * 65
Why We Oppose Votes for Men * Alice Duer Miller * 66
We Hate to See Them Go * Malvina Reynolds * 67
"We Hate to See Them Go" * Peggy Lipschutz * 68
War Preparers Anonymous * Kurt Vonnegut * 69
Messiah Arrives! * Not the Jewish Press * 71
St.Lawrence Island's Monster * Grace Cross Antoghame Akumelingekuk * 72
"The Earth is Our Mother" * Karl Jadrnicek * 75
The Paint Box * Tali Shurek * 76
Why the Baby Says "Goo-Goo" * Jiiva Kala * 77
Tickling the Baby * Nina Uccello * 78
The Dove and the Hawk * Fritz Eichenberg * 79
Affirmation * Nancy Schimmel * 80
"It Could Be a Wonderful World" * Peggy Lipschutz * Back Cover

My Rainbow Race
--Pete Seeger

One blue sky above us,
One ocean lapping all our shores,
One earth so green and round,
Who could ask for more?
And because I love you,
I'll give it one more try
To show my rainbow race
It's too soon to die.

Some folks want to be like an ostrich:
Bury their heads in the sand...
Some hope for plastic dreams
to unclench all those greedy hands...
Some want to take the easy way: Poisons, bombs!
They think we need 'em.
Don't they know you can't kill all the unbelievers?
There's no shortcut to freedom.

Go tell, go tell all the little children!
Go tell mothers and fathers, too:
Now's our last chance to learn to share
what's been given to me and you.

One blue sky above us,
One ocean lapping all our shores,
One earth so green and round,
Who could ask for more?

© 1970, 1972 by SANGA MUSIC, Inc.
All rights reserved
Used by Permission

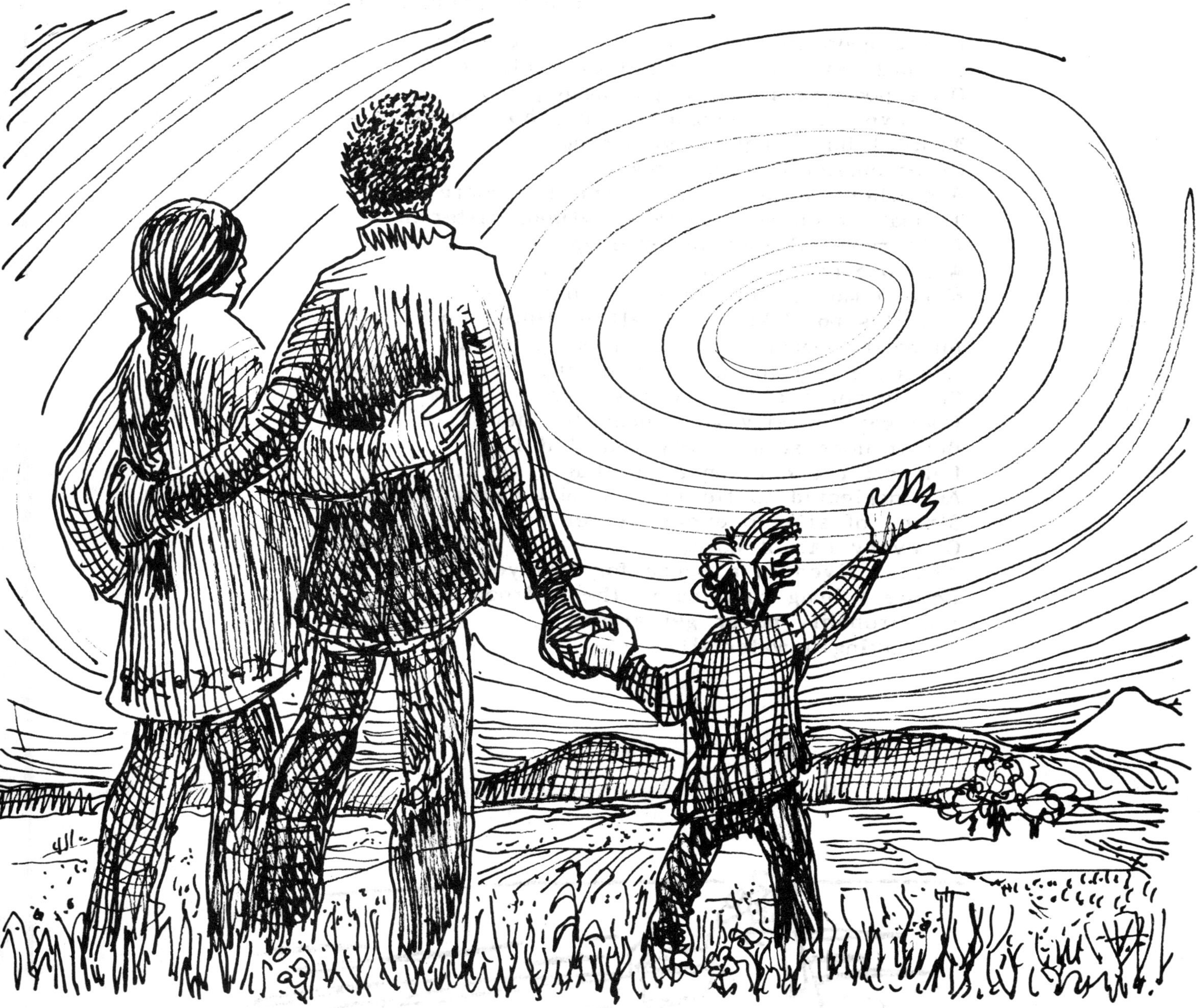

It's a Good Thing I'm Not in Charge Here

--Evi Seidman
Eureka Springs, Arkansas

It's a good thing I'm not in charge here.
I could never have thought of a pine cone
Or a pomegranate or a porcupine,
And even if I'd thought of one, how on earth
Would I have engineered a comet
Or organized life in a pond,
And where would I have found the energy
To make each and every snowflake different
(It's more like me to come up
With one or two passable models,
Make a mold, and crank 'em out)
And it's not like me at all to finish up
An entire mountain range, then go back
And carefully touch up with tiny forests of moss
On the north side of every stone.
I've got a pretty good head for details
But it does seem likely that I'd have
Left off the dots on a ladybug's back,
And neglected to tie in each and every
Strand of silk to every kernel
Of every ear of corn;
Why, I lived in a house for two years
Before I hung curtains in the bedroom--
I'd probably never get around
To making a waterfall.

The Story of Sadako Sasaki

In Hiroshima, in 1943, a little girl was born whose name was Sadako Sasaki. When she was two years old, the U.S.A. dropped a nuclear bomb on Hiroshima. Many innocent people died. Sadako lived, but, like many other children, some of them still inside their mothers' bodies, she got a little particle of that radioactive material inside her body. (This is the same material that is released from nuclear power plants in their routine "safe" emissions.)

She had a happy, normal life until she was twelve years old, in the fifth grade, and she could run like the wind. Her class chose her as their representative in the relay races. She could run very fast!

One day, after school, she practiced her running, and, on the way home, saw the moon rising over the horizon. She remembered a song she had sung when she was much smaller, and sang it to the moon:

> "Sho, sho, sho-jo-ji,
> Sho-jo-ji no-ni-wa-wa,
> Too, too, too-ki-yo-ni,
> Mina-deh-deh koi-koi-koi!"

"The moon is bright,
The night is beautiful,
Come, and sing, and dance with me!
Come, come, come!"

The next day, she again went to school, and again practiced her running. As she was running, Sadako fainted, and was taken to the hospital. In the hospital, they told her that she had leukemia, the nuclear bomb disease. Many children in and around Hiroshima and Nagasaki had gotten leukemia seven, eight, ten years after the bomb had dropped. Some had still been inside their mothers' bodies when the bomb was dropped, and were only six or seven years old when they found out they had leukemia. This was why it was called the atomic bomb disease.

You can imagine being twelve years old, in the fifth grade, and finding out that you have leukemia. Sadako didn't want to die, she wanted to have a long and happy life. One of her friends came to visit her in the hospital, and folded a gold square of paper into a paper crane, oritsuru, saying, "The paper crane represents long and happy life, and, it is said, if you fold a thousand paper cranes you will be assured of a long and happy life."

Sadako's family and friends brought her paper squares of all different colors, and she folded them into cranes. Her brother hung them from the ceiling of the hospital bedroom, and brightened the room up, making it truly beautiful. Sometimes her fingers moved with all fluidity, and it was easy to fold. Sometimes, she would have arthritic pains, but Sadako still folded because she knew that if she reached a thousand, she would be cured of the leukemia, and have a long and happy life.

On a certain day, she sensed that a cure was not possible; she would never get well. She continued to fold the cranes, but her prayer was no longer for recovery from her illness, but of health and peace for all the people of the world. As she finished each crane, she addressed a short litany to the little paper crane, "I will write peace on your wings and you will fly all over the world." After folding 644 cranes, on the twenty-fifth of October, 1955, Sadako died in the Hiroshima Red Cross Hospital. Her family, the students at Noborimachi Junior High School, and children all over Japan, and later, the world, mourned for Sadako.

The children of Japan collected money to build a monument to Sadako Sasaki and all the other children who died from the A-bomb. The monument has a statue of Sadako holding a large golden crane over her head. At the base of the statue are the words:

"This is our cry,
This is our prayer:
Peace in the world!"

People come from all over the world and hang paper cranes from the statue. Sometimes, people will send a paper crane, or a string of paper cranes, or even just tell the story of Sadako, to their government leaders, telling them, "We want all the children of the world to have long and happy lives. Stop making nuclear power plants, and preparing for nuclear war. This is not a way to assure children of having long and happy lives. Our cry and our prayer is also for Peace in the world."

The Adventures of a Little Sparrow
--Yukari Kadoguchi

(translated by Scott and Motoko Hori Foster)

Once upon a time there was a little sparrow who had only left the nest a short time before. He knew nothing about the world. One morning he said to himself, "I want to get out of this bamboo thicket."

So the next day he flew away, often stopping to rest, until he smelled something good and flew down to see what it was. He landed in a rice field where the heavy heads of the ripe grain were hanging down all around. The little sparrow ate like crazy until he was stuffed. Then he looked up and noticed something strange standing on one leg. "What on earth is that?" he wondered. He flew up and pecked the scarecrow's face.

"Aren't you afraid of me, little sparrow?" said the scarecrow.

The little sparrow shook his head no and asked him, "Who are you?"

"I'm a scarecrow. You must be a new sparrow," he laughed.

The little sparrow looked doubtful and asked, "Why should I be afraid of you?"

The scarecrow smirked, "You'll see."

So the little sparrow flew off until he found what he thought was a bigger scarecrow. "Hello, big scarecrow!" he said confidently.

"I'm not a scarecrow, kid," the big one answered in a deep voice.

"But you're standing on one leg," said the little sparrow.

"I am, but I had two good legs before."

"Well, who are you?" asked the little sparrow again, puzzled.

"I am a Torii, a gateway at the entrance to a Shinto shrine."

"Then why are you pretending to be a scarecrow?"

"I'm not pretending. It wasn't my idea to be standing here on only one leg. People did this to me."

"People?" the little sparrow asked.

"It was an atomic bomb made by people that made me so ugly," whined the Torii pitifully.

The little sparrow remained quite unruffled and asked, "An atomic bomb, what's that?"

The Torii got a little irritated and said, "You know nothing."

So the little sparrow explained, "I know nothing because I just flew out of a bamboo thicket this morning. You shouldn't be surprised that I'm ignorant."

"Oh, I see," said the Torii. "Then why don't you go see the big old camphor tree and ask him? He knows something about everything, and he'll tell you everything."

"Thank you very much, Uncle Torii."

The little sparrow hopped to the camphor tree and perched on a thick branch. "Old tree! Old tree!" he called loudly.

"What is it, you noisy kid? You're interrupting my pleasant nap," the old tree said sleepily.

"I'm sorry I woke you up," said the little sparrow, "but I have to ask you something. Could you tell me what an atomic bomb is?"

"Don't you know what an atomic bomb is, kid?"

"Please tell me. I know nothing about the world."

"Well, ok, I'll explain it to you, kid. The atomic bomb is the second most frightening thing in the world. That Torii lost its leg because of it. And I was made ugly by it. You see my ugly color. In the past I was a tree thick with green leaves all year and people enjoyed my shade. That was my gift to them."

The little sparrow interrupted, "But that terrible atomic bomb was made by people, wasn't it?"

"Don't get excited," said the camphor tree. "Take the time to listen to me carefully. It was people who made the frightening atomic bomb and therefore I'm telling you that people are the most frightening thing in the world. They were ungrateful to me for giving them shade and they changed me into such a pitiful thing..."

"People are so frightening!" said the little sparrow, trembling with fear.

"They are certainly frightening, but they also killed themselves with their invention. They are more stupid than frightening."

"You mean they are stupid and frightening?"

"They can be bright, too. No matter how you look at it, they invent many good and clever things."

"Many things?" asked the sparrow.

"Yes. For example, they make houses and, come to think of it, this shrine. And those scarecrows you don't like."

"What? They made scarecrows, too?" The little sparrow became even more afraid and drew in his wings.

"So you kids have to be careful," said the old tree. "Scarecrows won't eat you, but there are people who will eat you."

"I understand. Well, then, tell me what people look like," demanded the little sparrow.

"You've seen a scarecrow, haven't you?"

"Yes, I have."

"Well, imagine a scarecrow with two legs. And they can move around. Furthermore, they have two hands and a head, which they can also move. Listen to me carefully. Never approach them. They also have what they call tools and weapons. But they can't fly, so when you see them, fly away as quickly as possible. Nothing good will ever come of approaching them carelessly," the old tree warned seriously.

"I think I should go back to the bamboo thicket soon," said the little sparrow. "I wouldn't stay with people for the world. I might lose my leg accidentally, too."

The old tree heard the little sparrow's resolve and said in a sleepy voice, "That's a good decision, kid. I'll go back to sleep now. Go back to your nest, and be careful." And the tree began to snore.

"Good-bye, good-bye, old tree," said the little sparrow, flying up into the sky and back to the bamboo thicket at full speed.

Since then, the little sparrow has always gone back to the bamboo thicket to sleep where there are no people. And when he looks up at the sky and sees a towering thundercloud, he remembers the old tree's story of the terrible atomic bomb and he is startled even by the rustling of the bamboo leaves.

(This story was given by Fusako Kurahara, of ASSITEJ/Japan, (International Association of Theater for Young People.) The publisher, Masao Araki, was glad to see its story going forth. It is recommended that the adult finish off the story by reminding the child that the sparrow can do nothing about creating peace, but we human beings can do a great deal by doing fewer "stupid and frightening" things, and more "good and clever" actions.)

The Diary of Anne Frank

(Anne Frank received a diary on her thirteenth birthday, and, very soon afterwards, went into hiding in Amsterdam. The hiding place, consisting of six small rooms, was a home for two years to Anne, her mother, father, sister, and four other Jews who wanted to escape death at Nazi hands. Her diary stops two days before their hiding place is invaded by the Gestapo, in July of 1944, and she died a few months later at the concentration camp in Bergen-Belsen. Her father, the only survivor of the group, found the diary after the war. In these two entries, she speaks to Kitty, her diary, translated here from the Dutch by B.M. Mooyaart-Doubleday, on Wednesday, the third of May, and Saturday, the fifteenth of July, 1944, and tells of her views on war and peace.)

Wednesday, 3rd May, 1944

Dear Kitty,

First, just the news of the week. We're having a holiday from politics; there is nothing, absolutely nothing to report. I too am gradually beginning to believe that the invasion will come. After all, they can't let the Russians clear up everything; for that matter, they're not doing anything either at the moment.

Mr. Koophuis comes to the office every morning again now. He's got a new spring for Peter's divan, so Peter will have to do some upholstering, about which, quite understandably, he doesn't feel a bit keen.

Have I told you that Moffi has disappeared? Simply vanished--we haven't seen a sign of him since Thursday of last week. I expect he's already in the cats' heaven, while some animal lover is enjoying a succulent meal from him. Perhaps some little girl will be given a fur cap out of his skin. Peter is very sad about it.

Since Saturday we've changed over, and have lunch at half-past eleven in the mornings, so we have to last out with one cupful of porridge; this saves us a meal. Vegetables are still very difficult to obtain: we had rotten boiled lettuce this afternoon. Ordinary lettuce, spinach and boiled lettuce, there's nothing else. With these we eat rotten potatoes, so it's a delicious combination!

As you can easily imagine we often ask ourselves here despairingly: "What, oh what is the use of war? Why can't people live peacefully together? Why all this destruction?"

The question is very understandable, but no one has found a satisfactory answer to it so far. Yes, why do they make still more gigantic 'planes, still heavier bombs and, at the same time, prefabricated houses for reconstruction? Why should millions be spent daily on the war and yet there's not a penny available for medical services, artists, or for poor people?

Why do some people have to starve, while there are surpluses rotting in other parts of the world? Oh, why are people so crazy?

I don't believe that the big men, the politicians and the capitalists alone are guilty of war. Oh, no, the little man is just as keen, otherwise the people of the world would have risen in revolt long ago! There is an urge and rage in people to destroy, to kill, to murder, and until all mankind, without exception, undergoes a great change, wars will be waged, everything that has been built up, cultivated and grown, will be destroyed and disfigured, after which mankind will have to begin all over again.

Seed Corn Must Not Be Ground
 -- Käthe Kollwitz

I have often been downcast, but never in despair; I regard our hiding as a dangerous adventure, romantic and interesting at the same time. In my diary I treat all the privations as amusing. I have made up my mind now to lead a different life from other girls and, later on, different from ordinary housewives. My start has been so very full of interest, and that is the sole reason why I have to laugh at the humorous side of the most dangerous moments.

I am young and I possess many buried qualities; I am young and strong and am living a great adventure; I am still in the midst of it and can't grumble the whole day long. I have been given a lot, a happy nature, a great deal of cheerfulness and strength. Every day I feel that I am developing inwardly, that the liberation is drawing nearer and how beautiful nature is, how good the people are about me, how interesting this adventure is! Why, then, should I be in despair?

Yours,

Anne

Saturday, 15th July, 1944

(...)
"For in its innermost depths youth is lonelier than old age." I read this saying in some book and I've always remembered it, and found it to be true. Is it true then that grown-ups have a more difficult time here than we do? No. I know it isn't. Older people have formed their opinions about everything, and don't waver before they act. It's twice as hard for us young ones to hold our ground, and maintain our opinions, in a time when all ideals are being shattered and destroyed, when people are showing their worst side, and do not know whether to believe in truth and right and God.

Anyone who claims that the older ones have a more difficult time here, certainly doesn't realise to what extent our problems weight down on us, problems for which we are probably much too young, but which thrust themselves upon us continually, until, after a long time, we think we've found a solution, but the solution doesn't seem able to reduce the facts which reduce it to nothing again. That's the difficulty in these times: ideals, dreams, and cherished hopes rise within us, only to meet the horrible truth and be shattered.

It's really a wonder that I haven't dropped all my ideals because they seem so absurd and impossible to carry out. Yet, I keep them, because in spite of everything I still believe that people are really good at heart. I simply can't build up my hopes on a foundation consisting of confusion, misery, and death. I see the world gradually being turned into a wilderness, I hear the ever-approaching thunder, which will destroy us too, I can feel the sufferings of millions and yet, if I look up into the heavens, I think that it will all come right, that this cruelty too will end, and that peace and tranquillity will return again.

In the meantime, I must uphold my ideals, for perhaps the time will come when I shall be able to carry them out.

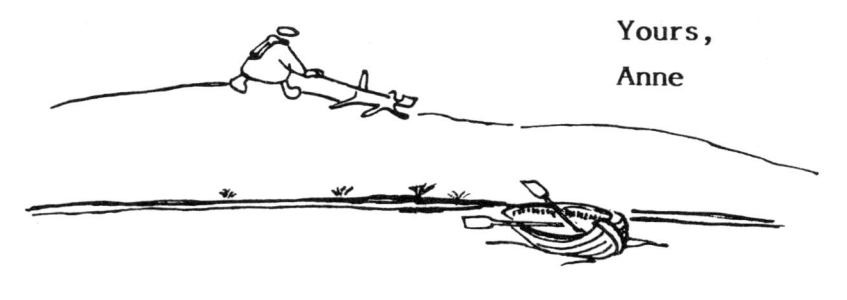

Yours,

Anne

The Quaker's Stroke

The Friends, or Quakers, believe in putting their actions behind their words: in witnessing for the tenets of Peace by doing and showing others courage and being actively pacific.

Well, once upon a time there was a Friend on board a U.S.A. trading vessel when a French privateer came up and gave them battle. Everyone on board the trading vessel except the Friend fought desperately for their lives. The Quaker, with his hands clasped behind his back, walked calmly and quietly up and down the deck, in the midst of the bullets.

Then the vessels came to close quarters, and the French cried out that they would soon board the US ship. The Quaker continued his constitutional. The sides of the ships bumped and grunted together. There was a loud shout of triumph from the French. The trading vessel's sailors loaded their guns and stood ready to sell their lives dearly. The captain of the privateer ship rushed forward to lead the attack, leaping from one ship's deck onto that of the trading vessel.

Just as he reached the trading vessel, and before anybody quite knew what had happened, the Quaker suddenly slipped up to him, put his arms around the Frenchman's body, and said calmly and reprovingly, "Friend, thou hast no business here." With that, he lifted up the French captain, and, as though he were handing a baby to its mother, dropped him gently but surely over the ship's side.

The wise know how to teach,

The fool how to smite. --Rabindranath Tagore

(from <u>Fireflies</u>)

The White Crane Woman
--a story from China

(In the creation of peace, enormous amounts of valor and self-assurance are and will be necessary for those who choose life for all the living beings of the world. Physical, mental, emotional, and spiritual strength can be given in a subtle manner through a story of sufficient mythic power and positivity. We, the soft, warm human beings (like this story's feather) can and will overcome the cold, hard bombs produced by the military mind (similar to this story's boulder) of the world. Bhavanii shared this story just before leaving to study to become a renunciate sister of Ananda Marga. Please pass on the story of the White Crane Woman:)

There was once a little girl, sitting at her bedroom window, looking out over the frozen rice fields, and up into the dark, cloudy skies, when she suddenly saw a bit of white in the distance. She watched as it came closer, and closer, and then recognized it as a white crane, flying, the only bit of beauty on a grey day. The little girl watched the crane, saw it come to a large boulder, and thought, "Oh, the crane will just fly around the boulder." Instead, the crane's wingtip feather touched the boulder, and the boulder rolled over. She watched as the crane flew away, and then thought to herself, "How is it possible for one white crane's wingtip feather to move a boulder? How can one feather move a boulder?"

The little girl did her work around the house, and thought about this question. She thought about it while she played, and it was the last thing she thought of before going to sleep that night: "How is it possible for one feather, one white wingtip feather of a crane to move a boulder?", and she fell asleep.

As she slept, she dreamt, and in her dream she saw two cranes fly in through her bedroom window, land on the floor, and become two very old people. They walked up to her bed and said, "We are the White Crane People, and we can teach you the answer to your question. But, you must decide, since it will take several years, whether you want to stay here, and lead a normal life, or do you want to go with us, and live with us for several years, and learn the answer to your question?" In her dream, she thought it over and said that she wanted to go with them, and learn the answer to her question.

In her dream, she felt herself being lifted, and, when she awoke, was no longer in the home of her family, in her own bed, but in a large bird's nest. Two very old people came up to her as she rubbed the sleep out of her eyes and said, "We are the White Crane People, and we will teach you the answer to your question, but you will have to live with us for several years."

So, she started to live with the White Crane People, and they taught her many interesting things: how to control the breath, how to move with grace, how to move quickly, but think calmly, how to immerse the mind in the thought of the Tao, the thought of limitlessness. And she practiced what they taught her until the teachings became part of her bones, part of her spirit.

After several years had passed, the Crane People came up to her and said, "Now we have taught you everything we can teach you; now, you know the answer to your question." But, even though they had taught her many interesting things, they had never spoken even once about how a crane's wingtip feather could move a boulder. Even though she had practiced all of these teachings until they were part of her, she didn't understand how it was possible for a white crane's wingtip feather to move a boulder. She felt confused, but knew better than to ask out loud. The White Crane People handed her a bowl of tea.

She knew what to do. She swirled the tea around, making a tiny tornado of tea leaves. When the tea leaves settled down, she gazed down, through the tea, through the tea leaves, through the bottom of the teabowl, and saw her parents and the people of her village being attacked by people from another place. She knew she had to return. She handed the teabowl back to the White Crane People and, suddenly, apprehended the answer to her question.

She realized that the only way a crane's wingtip feather can move a boulder is if the crane is controlling its breath; is if the crane is moving gracefully; is if the crane is moving quickly, but thinking calmly; is if the crane has immersed its mind in the thought of the Tao, the thought of limitlessness. And she understood this as she handed the teabowl back to the White Crane People.

That night, as she slept, she felt herself being lifted once again, and she awoke, not in the large bird's nest, but in her own bed. (Though the bed seemed somewhat shorter since she had grown several inches during the time she had been with the White Crane People.) She rubbed her eyes, went running through the house, found her parents, and hugged her parents. She realized that what she had seen through the bottom of the teabowl was not what had already happened, but what might happen.

She began to teach her parents, and the people of her home village, the things she had learned with the White Crane People: how to control the breath, how to move gracefully, how to move quickly but think calmly, how to immerse the mind in the thought of the Tao.

The people took her instructions and made them into a system which we now call Karate, a gift of the White Crane Woman.

Hibakusha

The Determination of Men and Women
Is Greater Than the Strength of the A - Bomb.
-- Ittetsu Morishita

Mrs. Motoyo Fujiwara

(Born 1894; most recent photo, November, 1983)
(Located 680 meters from hypocenter at moment of Hiroshima bomb)

With a warm, carefree smile, Fujiwara-san welcomed photographer Ittetsu Morishita at a junior high school where she was working for daily wages under unemployment relief. She was sweeping up rhododendron petals. Boys and girls, three or four years younger than her son when he died from the atomic bomb, were playing there. She lost both her son and daughter to the bomb.

Her five-year-old daughter was with her mobilized for wartime labor. Her seventeen-year-old son worked by day and went to school at night. As usual, she had cooked rice over a simple charcoal burner and given him his lunch in a lunch box. She and her daughter were together when the bomb fell, and her daughter died on the second of September, less than a month after the bomb. Her son did not find his mother until three days after his sister had died. Then, two days later, he also died, coughing out fresh blood. She attended both of them in death.

Before dying, her son told her, "I'm going to die, but I'll guard you from the cares of life so that you may work healthily." From then on, she has lived a regular and orderly life, and even now, she cooks her rice and takes her lunch with her in a lunch box. At lunch time she thanks her son, and remembers her little daughter. After her meal, she takes a thirty minute rest, and then she washes the dishes.

Her table was made thirty years ago, by a soldier, a carpenter in civil life, who felt sorry for her without a table. She always polishes it. The soldier is dead now; he died, coughing blood, three days after working on it, she heard.

Looking at the style of life of this elderly lady with no gas range (She uses a coal stove), no television, etc., one gets the impression that she is living a life full of nostalgia for the old happy days with her children. Morishita-san could not help feeling that she is sustaining such a hard life with the convictin that any change in her lifestyle would be symbolic of further damage from the atomic bombing.

Though sometimes fatigued, she works well, but the memory of the atomic suffering never leaves her. The large keloid scars extending from her jaw to her chest are results of the injuries from the atomic blast that have not disappeared even now. Her hands, shoulders, and feet hurt terribly in the cold months of winter.

She finds courage in the memory of her son and daughter. She visits her family tomb three times a month, calmly joining her hands to salute the spirits of her children. Engraved on the tombstone is "Everybody meets in heaven." Her visit takes her past the stone Bodhisattva located at the former crematorium on the mountainside. Whenever she passes by it, the head has fallen, and she sets it up again.

The survivors of the atomic blast, such as Fujiwara-san, impart the impression by their lifestyles as well as by their determined attitudes not to let this happen again. Their sufferings teach us that such things should never happen again; they are actions unworthy of human beings.

SMBC LEISURE SERVICES IN CONJUNCTION WITH THE GREEN ROOM INVITES YOU TO JOIN

FLOATING EAGLE FEATHER

NATIVE AMERICAN STORY TELLER

MONDAY FEBRUARY 6TH — BROWSERS CLUB REDDISH LIBRARY GORTON RD REDDISH
6-7 PM DETAILS 432 2568

TUESDAY FEBRUARY 7TH — HAZEL GROVE LIBRARY BEECH AVE HAZEL GROVE
STORY TIME FOR 3 YR OLDS
11.00AM - 11.30AM DETAILS 483 6437

DIALSTONE LIBRARY LISBURNE LANE OFFERTON
3-5 yrs 2.15 - 2.45 pm DETAILS 483 2644

WEDNESDAY FEBRUARY 8TH — GREAT MOOR LIBRARY GLADSTONE STREET GREAT MOOR
10am - 11 am DETAILS 483 3092

THURSDAY FEBRUARY 9TH — HEALD GREEN LIBRARY FINNEY LANE HEALD GREEN
10am-11am DETAILS 437 3201

FRIDAY FEBRUARY 10TH — HEATON MOOR LIBRARY THORNFIELD ROAD HEATON MOOR
4.15 - 5pm DETAILS 432 5109

SATURDAY FEBRUARY 11TH — ROMILEY FORUM ROMILEY 10.30am - 11.30 am
ADMISSION 50P ON THE DOOR DETAILS 430 6570

SUNDAY FEBRUARY 12TH — THE GREEN ROOM 54-56 WHITWORTH STREET MANCHESTER
ADMISSION 2.00 ADULTS 1.50 CHILDREN.
2pm DETAILS 236 1677

MONDAY FEBRUARY 13TH — EDGELEY LIBRARY EDGELEY ROAD EDGELEY
2.30 - 3.00 pm DETAILS 480 4319

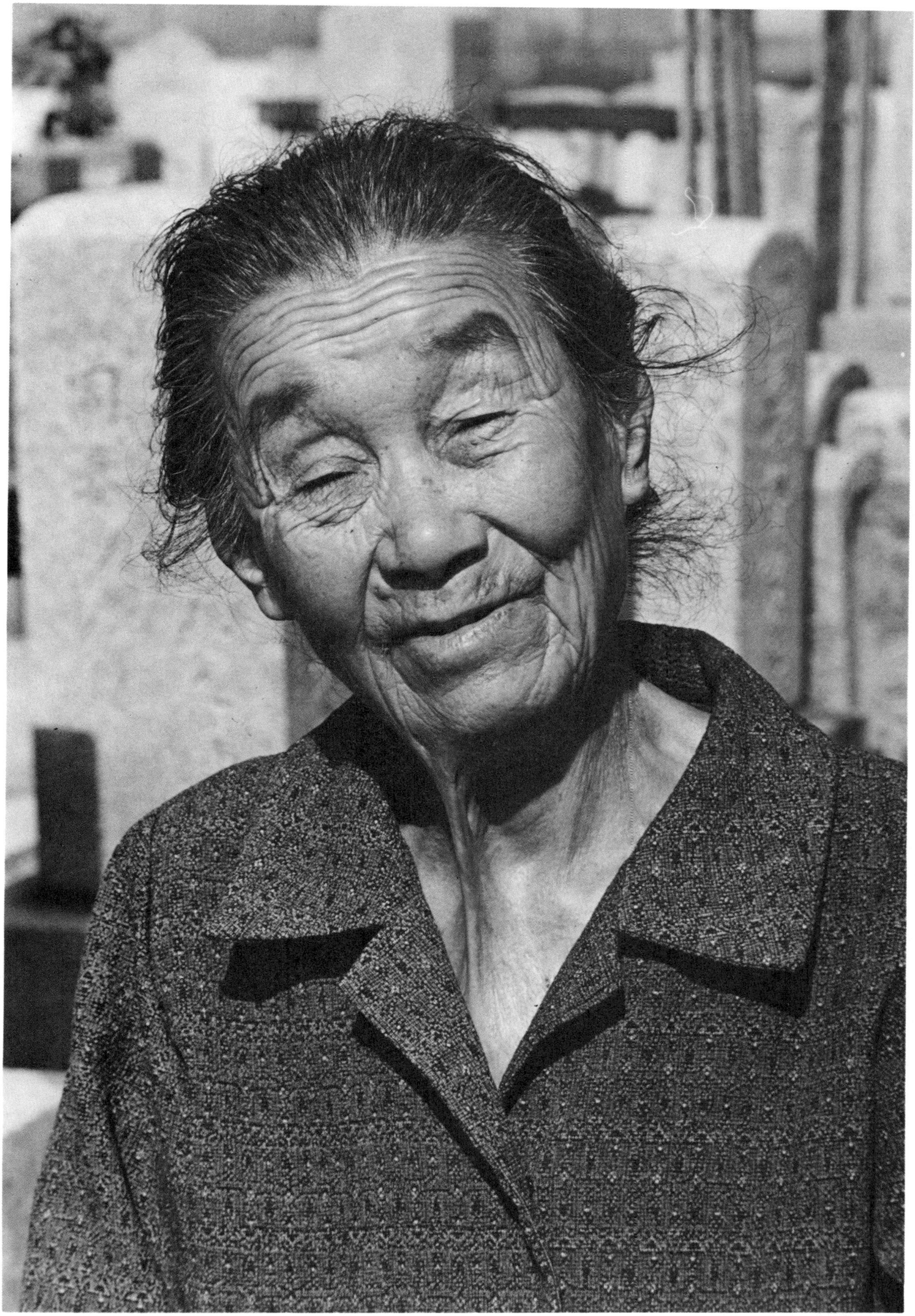

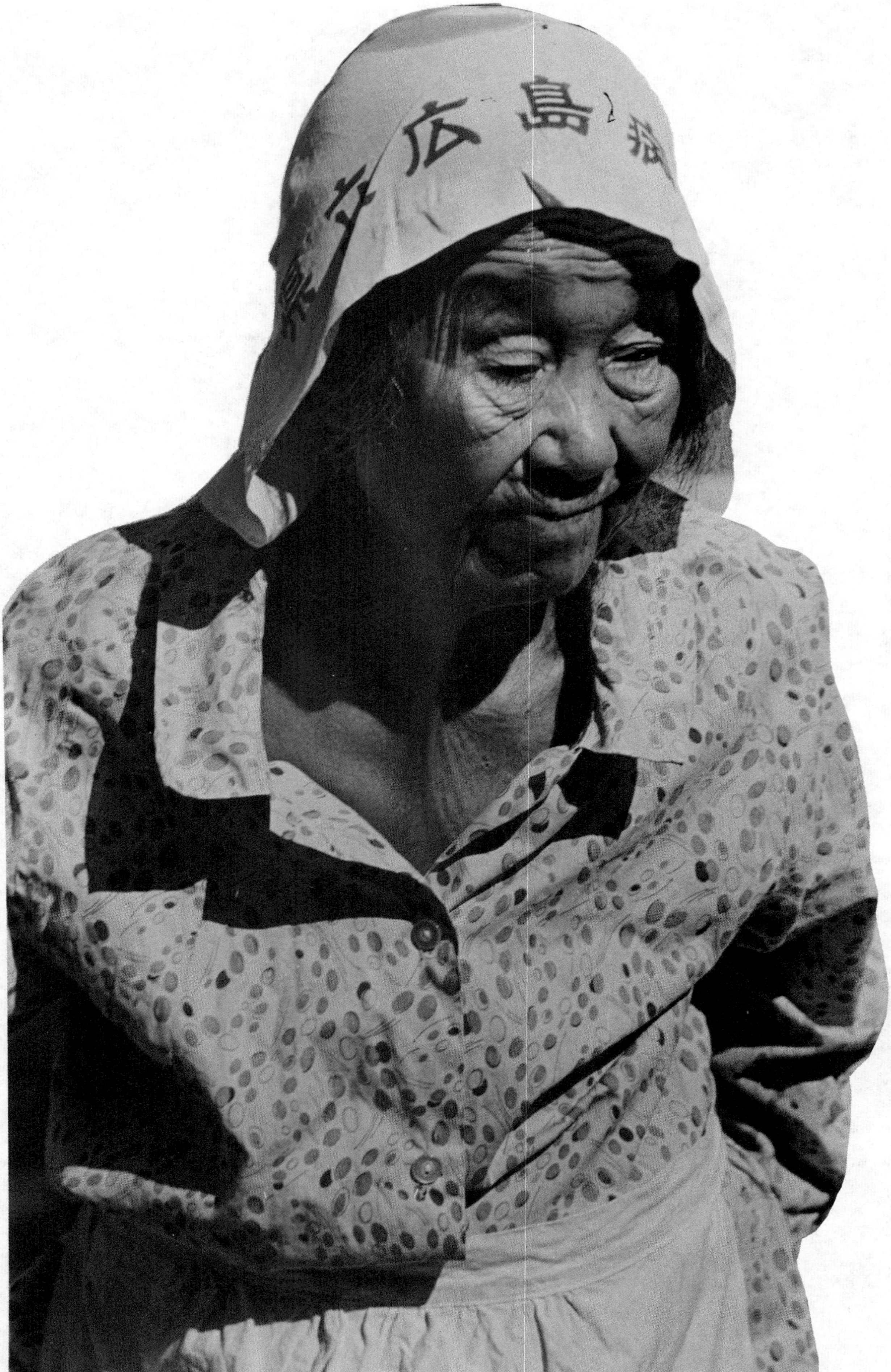
広島

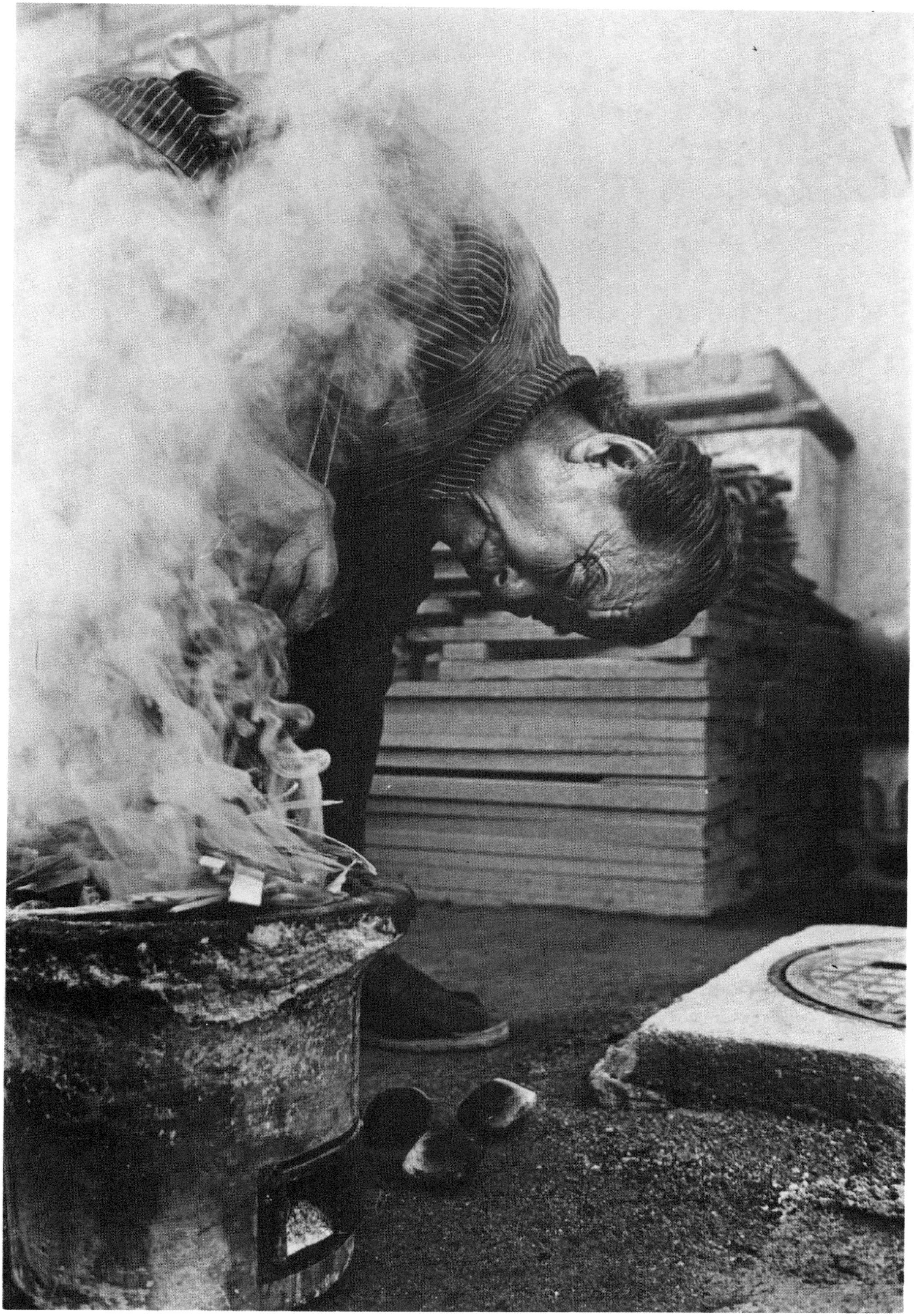

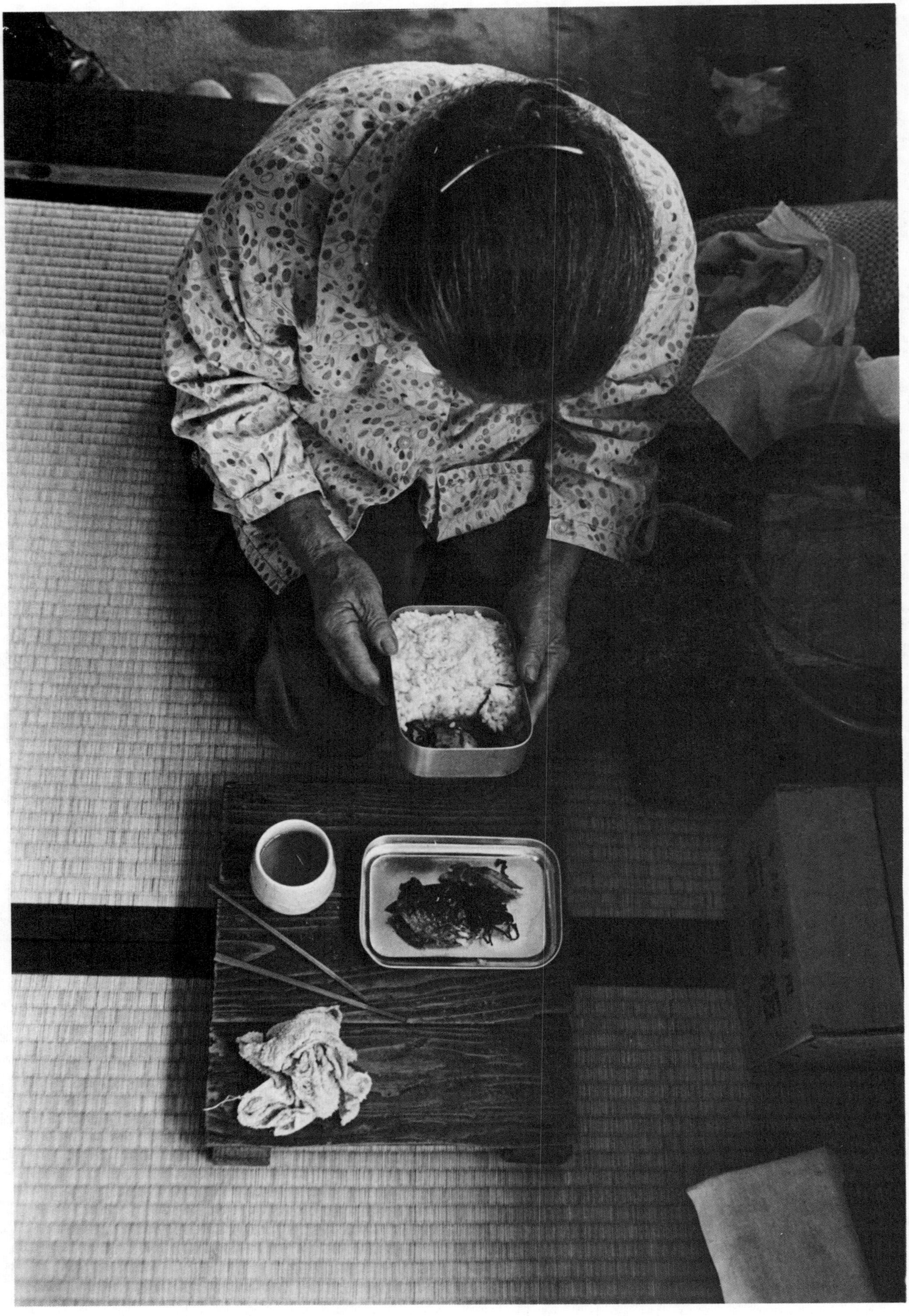

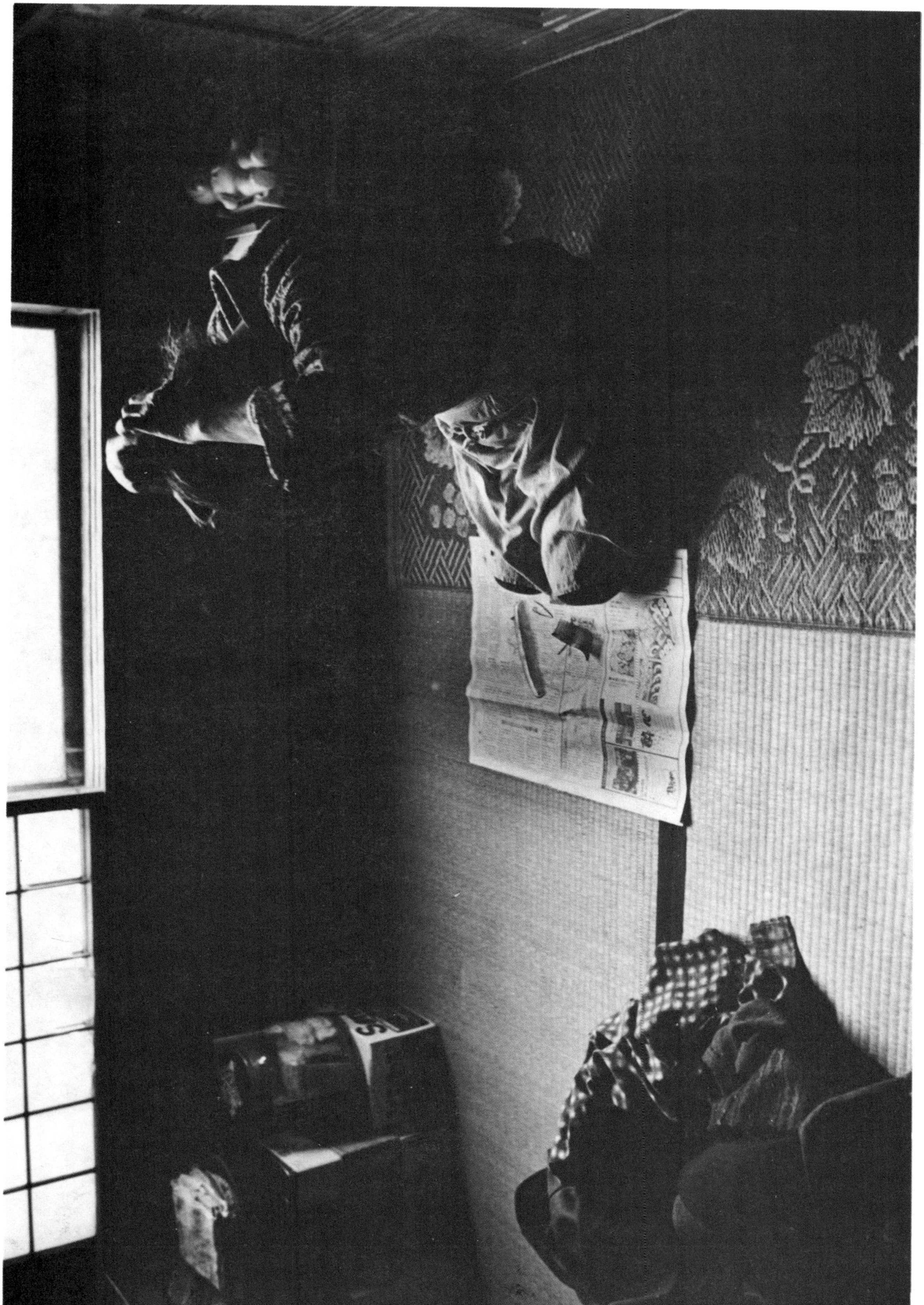

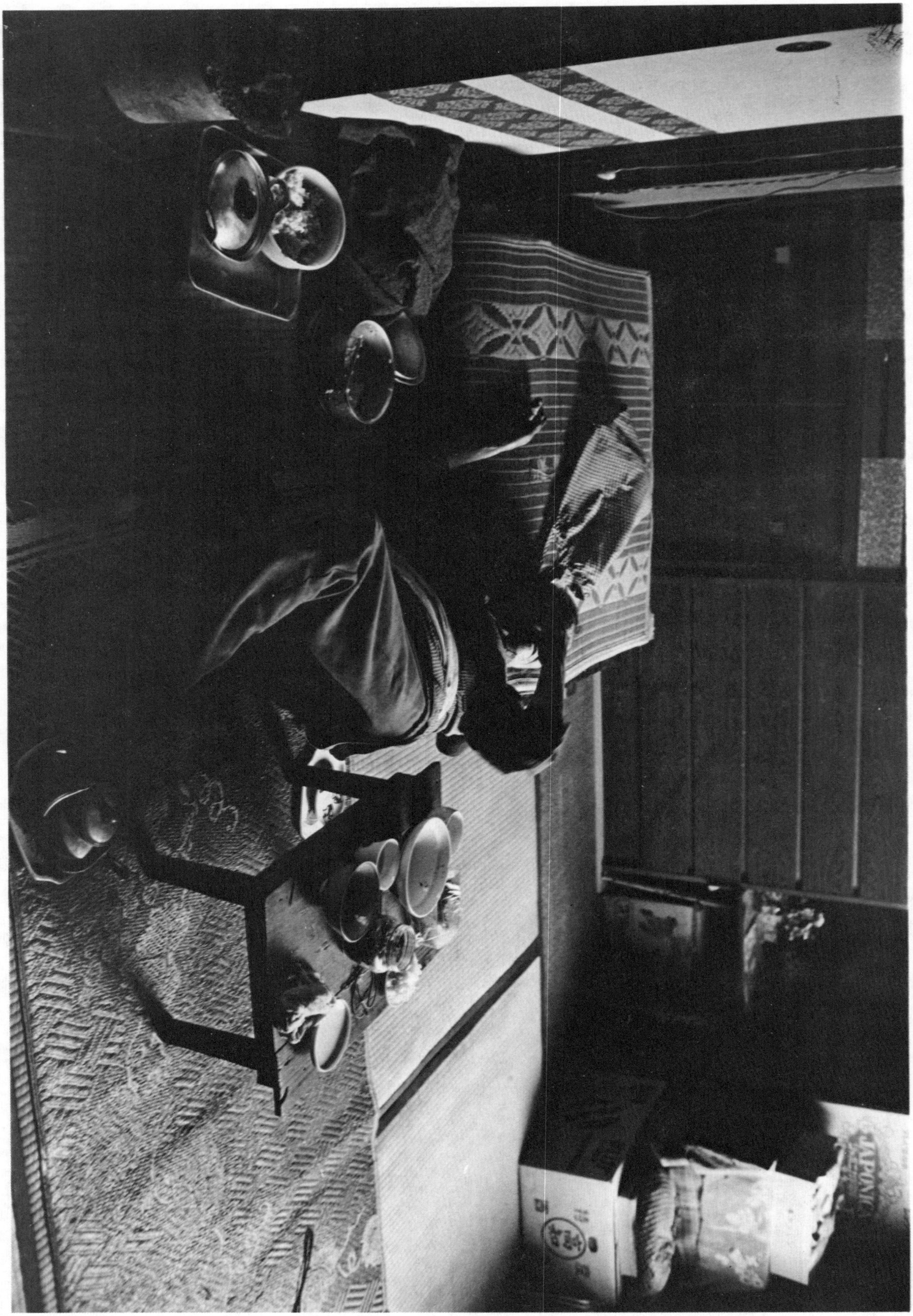

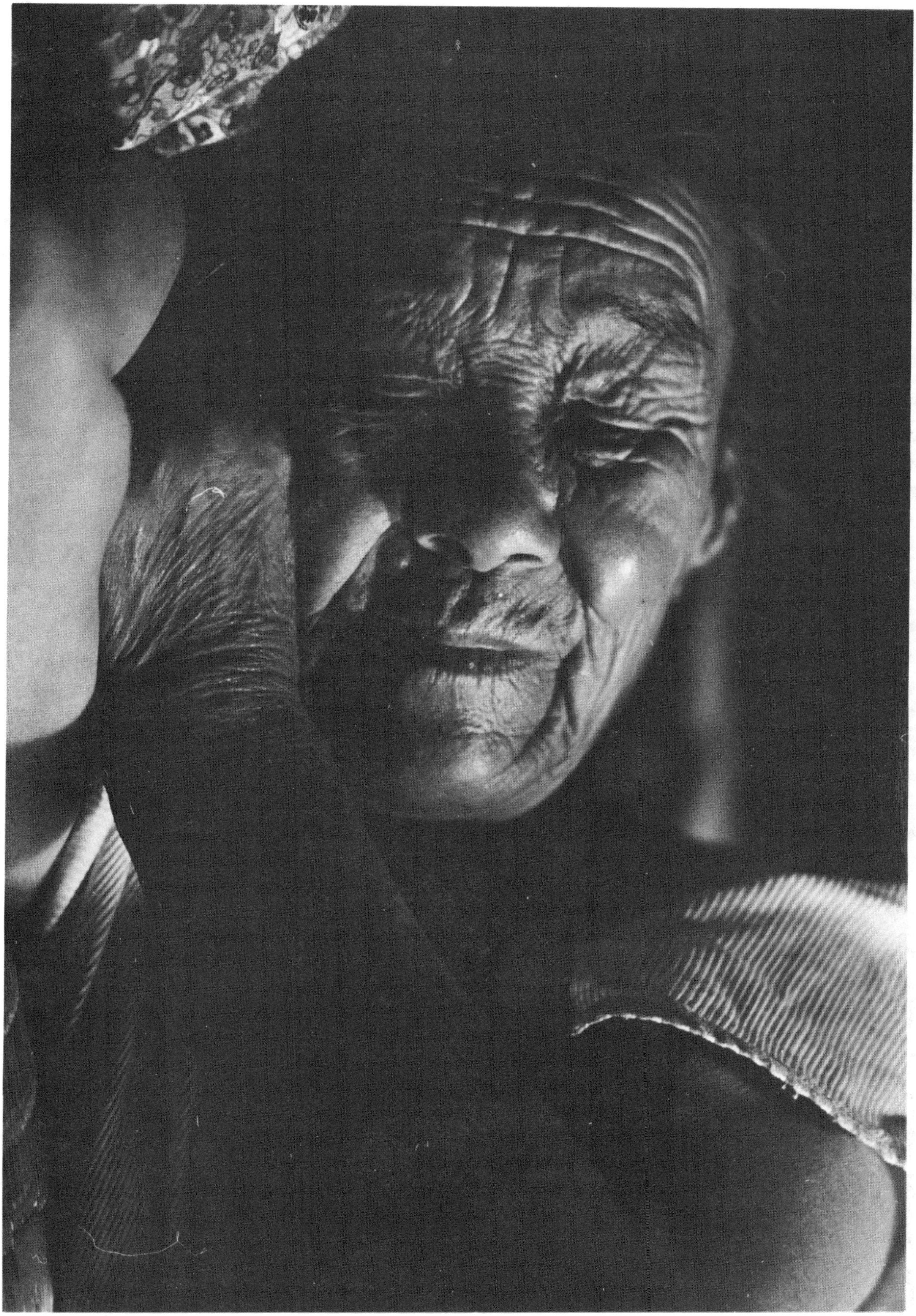

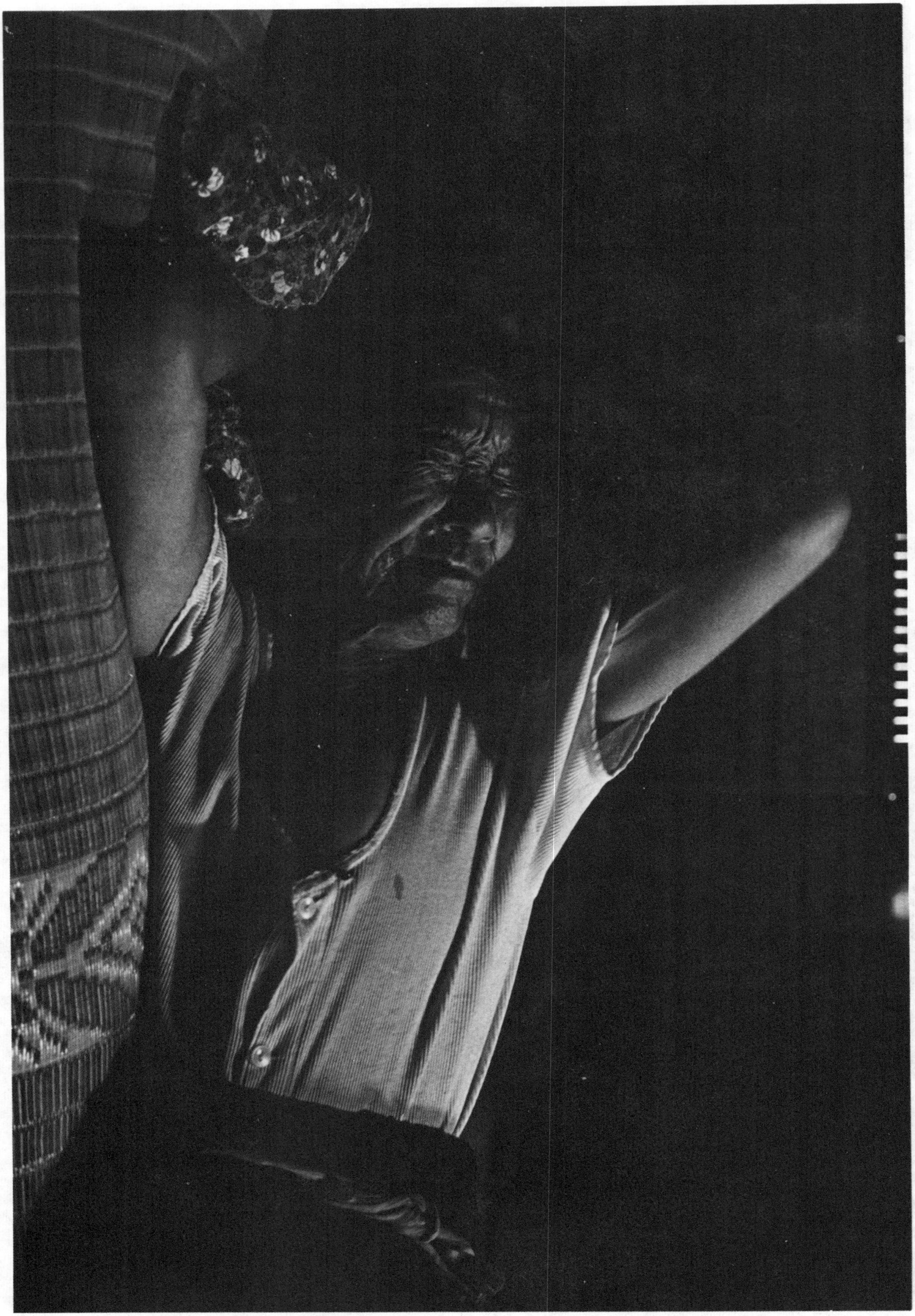

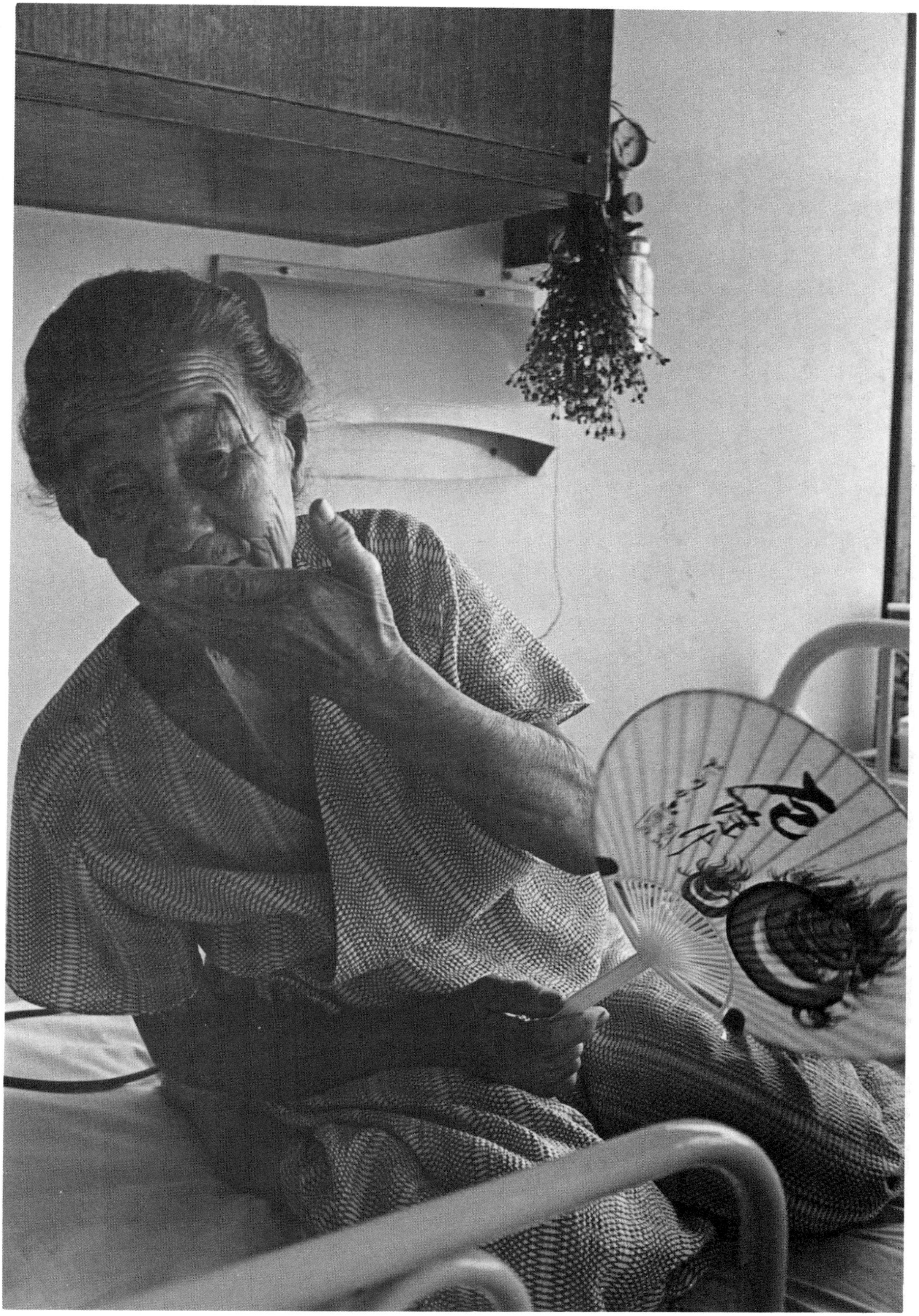

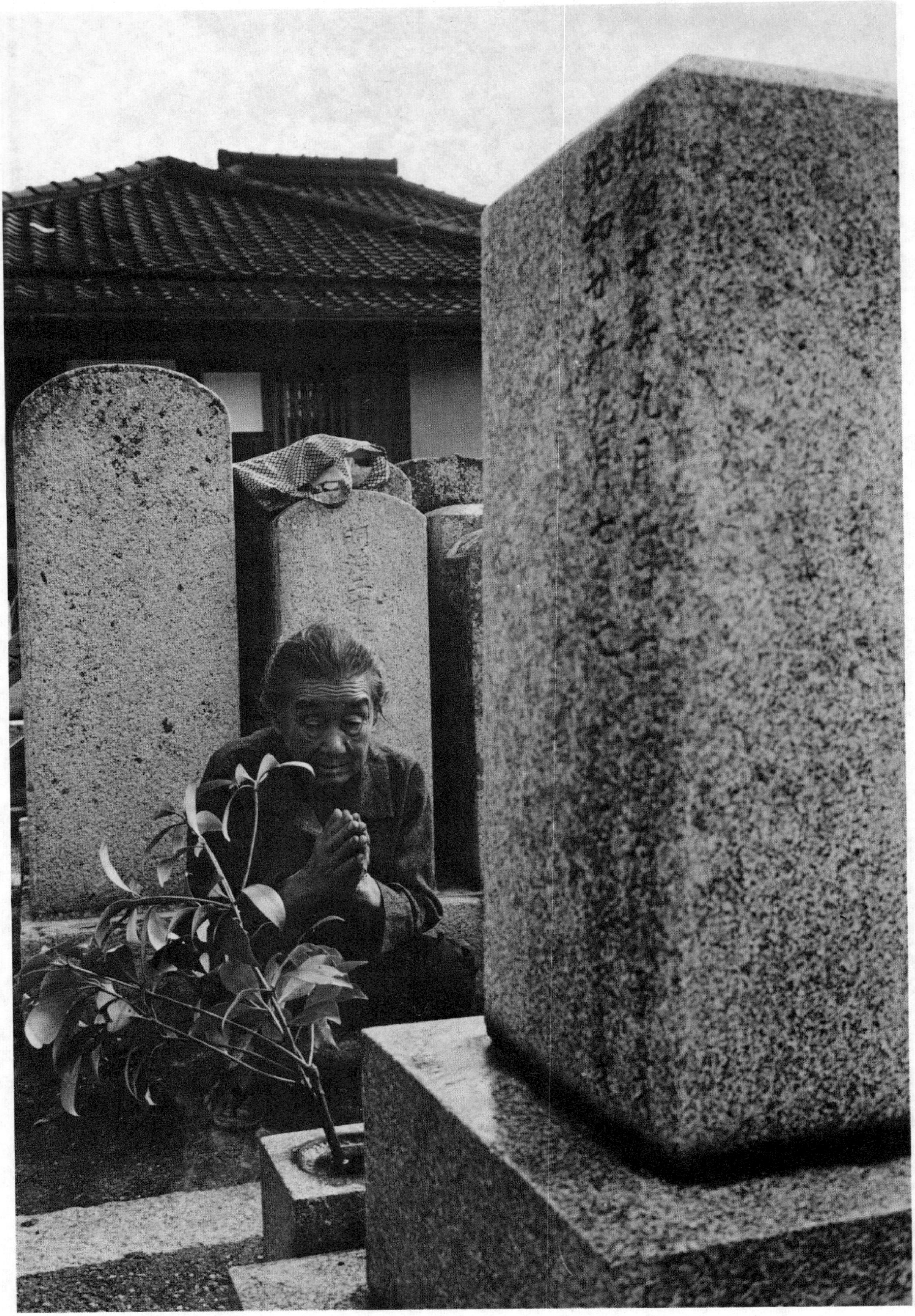

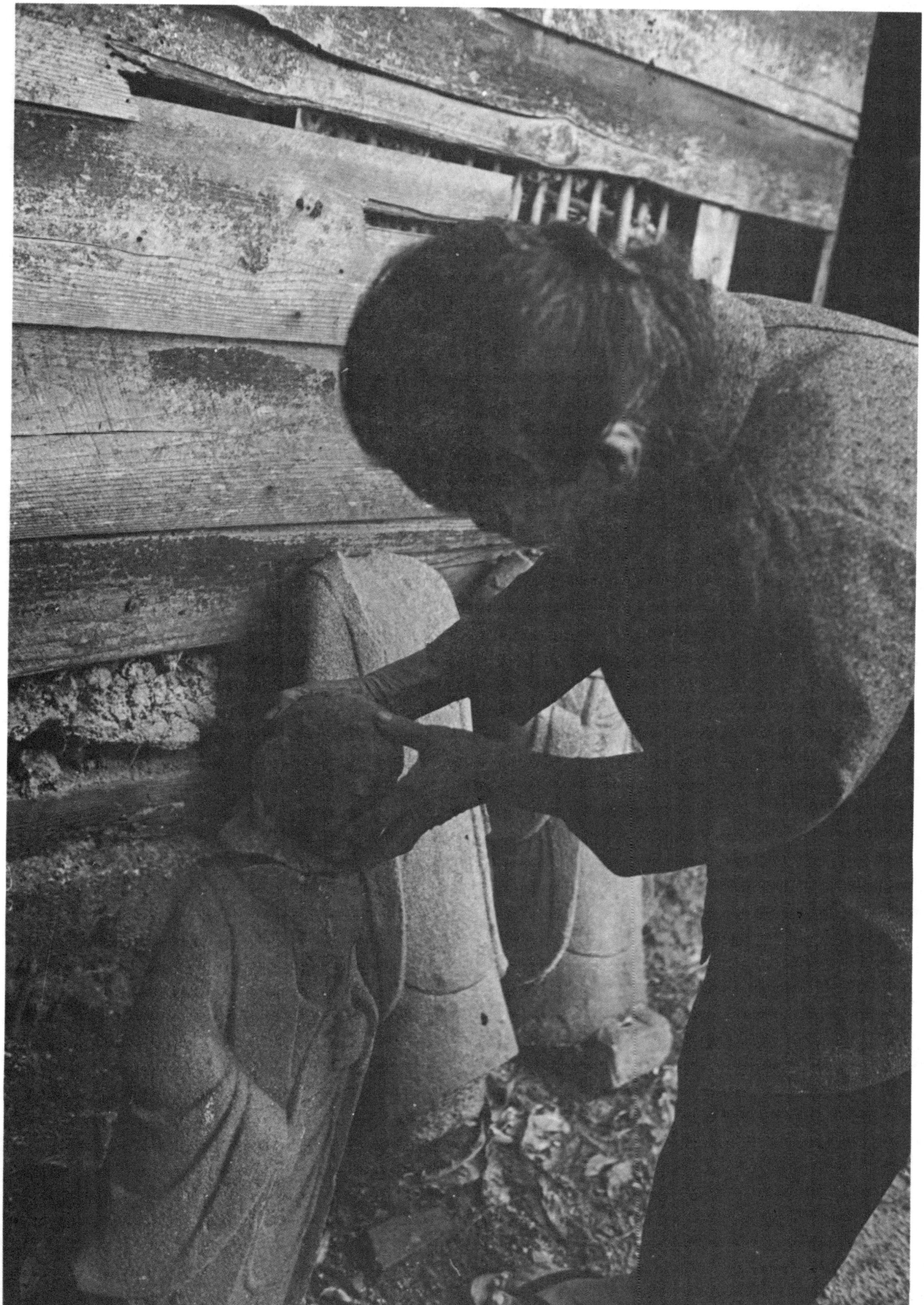

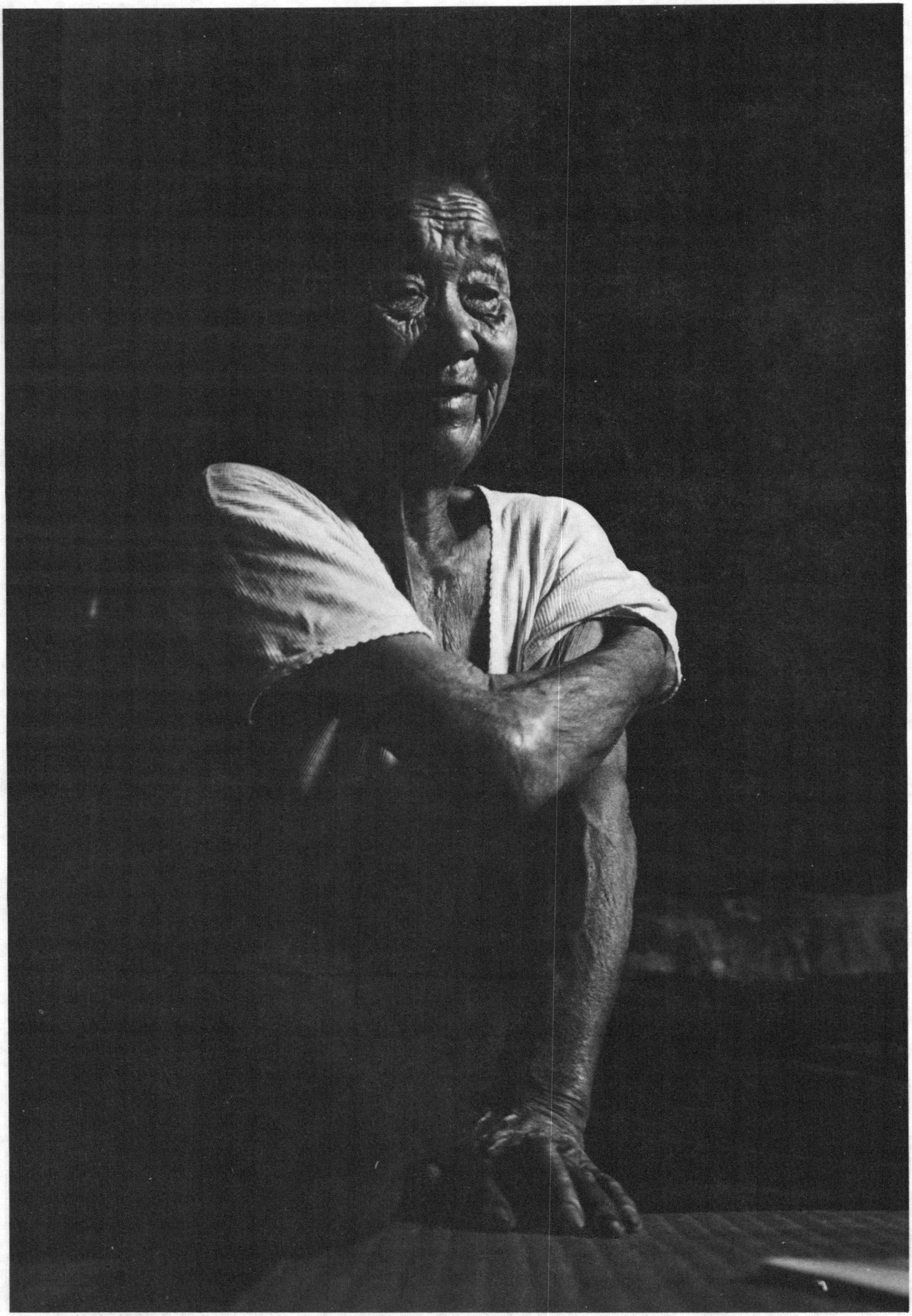

Sun Myth

--a Kathlamet traditional tale

(This Sun Myth was given by Rebecca Chamberlain-Fenwick, and is a myth which was recounted by a Kathlamet tribal member to Frank Boas in 1891. The story warns about something that may be beyond our power to understand or to control, as we have taken the nuclear power of the 93,000,000 mile distant sun and brought it dangerously close to ourselves. Shall we be able to make those who build and operate nuclear power plants and weapons stop before they senselessly destroy all of us?)

There was a chief of a town. His relatives lived in five towns. In the morning he used to go outside and stay out to look at the Sun. The Sun was about to rise. He said to his wife, "What would you think if I went to see the Sun?" She said to him, "Do you think the Sun is near that you want to go there?" On the following day he went out again. Again he saw the Sun. It was nearly sunrise. He said to his wife, "Make me ten pairs of shoes. Make me ten pairs of leggings." The woman made ten pairs of shoes and ten pairs of leggings. The next morning he went. He went far away. He used up his shoes and his leggings. Then he put on another pair of shoes and leggings. He went for five months. Then he had used five pairs of shoes and five pairs of leggings. He went for ten months. Then he was near the place where the Sun was rising and he had used all his shoes. Then he found a large house. He opened the door. There was a young woman. He entered and stayed there. He saw some arrows hanging on one side of the house. Quivers full of arrows were hanging there. There were hanging shirts of elk skin, wooden armor, shields, stone axes, bone clubs, and head ornaments. Implements used by men were hanging on the one side of the house. On the other side were mountain-goat blankets, dressed elkskin blankets, buffalo skins, dressed buckskins, long dentalia, short dentalia, and shell beads. Near the doorway some large thing was hanging. He did not know it. He asked the young woman, "Whose are these quivers?" "They are my father's mother's property. When I am grown up, she will give them away. Whose are these elkskin armors?" "They belong to my father's mother. When I am grown up, she will give them away." "Whose are these wooden armors?" "They belong to my father's mother. When I am grown up, she will give them away." "Whose are these shields and war clubs?" "They belong to my father's mother. When I am grown up, she will give them away." "Whose are these stone axes?" "They belong to my father's mother." Then also he asked about the things on the other side of the house: "Whose are these buffalo skins?" "They belong to my father's mother and to me. When I am grown up, she will give them away." "Whose are these mountain goat blankets?" "They belong to my father's mother. When I am grown up, she will give them away." "Whose are these dressed buckskins?" "They belong to my father's mother. When I am grown up, she will give them away." "Whose are these deerskin blankets?" "They belong to my father's mother. When I am grown up, she will give them away." "Whose are these shell beads?" "They belong to my father's mother. When I am grown up, she will give them away." "Whose are these long dentalia?" "They belong to my father's mother. When I am grown up, she will give them away." "Whose are these short dentalia?" "They belong to my father's mother. When I am grown up, she will give them away."

He asked about all those things, and thought: "I will take them." When it was evening, the old woman came home. She hung up something that pleased him. It was shining. He stayed there a long time and took that young woman. They remained there. Every morning the old woman disappeared. At night she came back. She brought home all kinds of things. She brought home arrows. Sometimes she brought mountain-goat blankets, and elkskin shirts. She did so every day. He stayed there a long time; then he grew homesick. For two days he did not rise. She asked her granddaughter: "Did you scold him and is he angry?" "No, I did not scold him; he is homesick." Then she asked her son-in-law: "What do you wish to have when you go home? Do you want these buffalo skins?" He said: "No." "Do you want these mountain-goat blankets?" He said: "No." "Do you want these elkskin shirts?" He said: "No." She showed him all that was on the one side of the house. Next she showed him the ornaments. She showed him everything. He liked that great thing that was hanging there. When that thing turned around it was shining so that one had to close one's eyes. That he wanted. He said to his wife: "The old woman shall give me only her blanket." His wife said to him: "She will not give it to you. The people tried to buy it, but she will not give it away." Then he became angry. After some days she asked him again: "Will you take this?" She showed him everything. She showed him all the implements used by men. When she came to that thing that was hanging there, she was silent. Then she became tired and said: "Take it, but look out if you carry it. You wanted it. I wished to love you and I do love you." Then she hung it onto him and she gave him a stone axe. She said: "Now go home." Now he went home.

He did not see a town until he came near his uncle's town. Now the thing which he carried in his hands shook, and said: "We shall strike your town." Then he lost his senses, and he broke his uncle's town and killed all the people. Now he recovered. He had broken all the houses. His hands were full of blood. Then he thought: "Oh, what a fool I was! The thing I wanted is bad." He tried to throw it away, but it stuck to his flesh. Then he went. He went a short distance and again he lost his senses. He came to the town of another one of his uncles. Again the thing said: "We shall strike your town." He tried to keep quiet, but he could not do it. He tried to throw it away, but his hands closed. Then he lost his senses, and broke all the houses. He recovered and the town of his uncle was destroyed. The people lay there dead. Then he cried and tried to strip it off in the fork of a tree, but it did not come off at all. It stuck to his body. He tried to strike what he wore on a stone, but he could not break it. Then he went on. He came near the town of another one of his uncles, and again the thing which he carried shook. "We shall strike your town," it said. Then he lost his senses. He broke the houses of his uncle's town. He destroyed his uncle's town. Then he recovered. He cried, because he made his relatives unhappy. He tried to dive in order to take it off, but it stuck to his body. He rolled himself in a thicket, and he tried to break on a stone what he wore. Then he gave it up. He cried. He went on and came to the town of another uncle. Again the thing which he carried shook: "We shall strike your town." He lost his senses. He broke all the houses and killed all the people. Then he recovered. All the people were killed, and the town was destroyed. His arms and his hands were covered with blood. He cried: "Kaa! kaa! kaa! kaa!" and tried to break what he wore on a stone, but it did not break. He tried to throw it away, but his hands closed. He went on, and he came near his own town. He tried to remain standing, but it was as if his feet were pulled toward it. Then he lost his senses and destroyed the whole town and killed his relatives. Then he recovered. The whole town was destroyed, and the ground was full of bodies. Then he cried again: "Kaa! kaa! kaa! kaa!" He bathed and tried to take off what he wore, but it stuck to his body. Sometimes he struck it against stones and thought it might get broken. Then he gave it up. He cried.

Now he looked back, and there the old woman was standing. She said to him: "I tried to love you; I tried to be kind to your people; why do you cry? You wished for it and wanted to wear my blanket." Now she took it off and left him. She went home. He stayed there; he went a short distance and built a small house.

Pearl Nakkai is the Dineh-Navajo woman standing next to the grave of her husband who died of lung cancer, a sickness unknown to the non-smoking Dineh, before uranium mining came to Shiprock, New Mexico. Her husband was a uranium miner. The uranium miners get lung cancer at six times the national average. The photo illustrates the hidden tragedy in the unharnessed and harmful desires to build nuclear weapons and power plants. It is a risk we all share. (Photograph by Geoff Manasse, 1978)

Warnings

--Holly Near

We believe in the warnings,
Warnings coming down
We believe that the living
Can turn this thing around

This is a celebration to see that we all are here
Time to express our anger, time to express our fear
And it doesn't mean that we all agree
Doesn't even mean we all are friends
But we believe in sweet Mother Earth
And her future we defend

Workers, you can guide us, Artists can sustain us
Children will outlive us
If we turn this thing around
Women bring in the living
And women sit with the dying
We'll find out if this is a birth or death
If we can turn this thing around

If you are a doctor, call radiation a crime
And if you are a healer, then come put your hand in mine
'Cause we believe in the warnings
Warnings coming down
We believe that the living
Can turn this thing around.

© 1979 Hereford Music
All rights reserved
Used by Permission

Fearlessness

(This story was told on a moon-less, star-filled night by a monk of Ananda Marga Yoga in Tiljala, India. May we become able to see the beauty of the night sky in all others around us!)

There was once a ghat, a burning place, where the bodies of the dead were taken for offering to the flames of the pyre, and many people had heard that it was haunted. It was said that no one who entered the portals of the ghat past sunset would see the light of the next day.

A man heard these rumors, and said, "God is everywhere! With this in mind, the ghat will be safe for me, I am sure." He decided to go to the ghat at sunset and stay there all night and see what would happen.

As the sun was setting, he went through the portals of the ghat, and sat down. He was confident, and felt all would be well. The sky started to darken, as the earth continued rotating the ghat away from the warm, cheery sunlight. The fellow started to feel jittery, and more and more frightened as the darkness descended. He started to hear a strange sound. He listened carefully, and knew it to be the sound of many children, crying. He knew it was the voices of the children's spirits coming to take him to join them. He stood.

"But wait," he thought, "maybe it's something else. Let me go toward the sound and see what is making it. He started walking towards the sound, and came to the edge of the ghat, where a large tree was growing, and on its huge branches, a group of vultures were calling. Their cries had sounded like the weeping of many children. Relieved, the man sat down once again.

Almost as soon as he sat down, he heard a new sound. It was the sound of breathing, heavy and faraway. This was not so bad, but the breathing was getting closer, and closer. He stood.

"But wait," he thought, "maybe it's something else. Let me go toward the sound and see what is making it." Walking, as before, towards the sound he had feared, he came to hollow bones, and skulls, through which the wind was blowing, and making a sound of hollow, strenuous breathing.

"Each time, I became frightened because my mind led me to believe in my unproven, and unfounded, fears. I became frightened because I thought I should be frightened. My mind did it, challenging my mind with itself undid it."

As he dropped his mind's fears into the flickering flames of a fire at the ghat, he suddenly was able to perceive the beauty of the night. He had been so filled with his fears about the sounds he had imagined hearing, that the night sky had not existed save as a backdrop for his imagined fears. Suddenly, the stars opened in front of him, and the clouds sailing across in all their diversity, and the crossed branches and silhouettes of vultures in the large tree at the edge of the ghat. He became lost in the ecstasy of watching the night sky, and fell safe and soundly asleep while delectating the night's beauties.

People were surprised to see him emerge the next day, happy and well. They still didn't go to the ghat at night, but now, it was without fear that they didn't go.

The Seventh Sister

--a folk story by the women of Greenham Common

(The peace camp of women at the gates of the USA Military Base in Greenham Common, England, has brought many people around the world strength and inspiration to work for peace, striving for the commitment to it that these women have given. This is a folk story invented one night to pass the time and weave their hearts closer.)

The women of the yellow gate were faced with a particularly surly bunch of police this morning. For two months, now, the police officers had come each morning to each gate and forced the women to vacate. They packed away their tents, fires, and awnings against the rain and sleet of winter, and left. As soon as the police leave, each time, the women return to their camps. The harassment occurs with some good-natured joking between the police and the women sometimes, but not this morning. As the women are vacating, a bucket of water is poured by one of the officers over the fire they had worked so hard to start on this cold, wet morning.

Now, among the stars the night before, among the Pleiades to be exact, the six sisters were concerned about the seventh sister. She was dim and blinking, and sometimes people on Earth even had a hard time telling there was a seventh star there. The six sisters finally decided to ask Seventh Sister if there was anything they could do -- why was she so out of sorts and dim?

"Well," she responded, "I've been hearing a lot about our sisters in Greenham Common, the commitment they've made to peace for all people, and I get so curious about them that I forget to glow brightly, as all of you do so nicely. I want to go and talk to them and see what they're like, see what their lives are like. Would all of you give me permission to go and see them?"

"Why, yes, what you say is a great idea," answer the other six sisters, "We also have been curious about them. Go and come back soon to tell us all you've learned."

Seventh Sister soared through the night skies, and reached the site of the camp at the yellow gate of Greenham Common soon after the women had come back. "It's no use! I've tried and tried to get this damp wood lit, but it is impossible," says Isia as Seventh Sister approaches. The women at yellow gate turn when they see the flash through the sky beside them; they are even more surprised when they hear a voice addressing them from the flames...

"Please, use the flames of my arrival to light your fire," says Seventh Sister.

Isia, a little befuddled, but remembering her duty as firekeeper at this moment, takes one of the dampened branches and approaches it to the flames rising from Seventh Sister. When the fire is burning brightly, all of the women turn their attention again to Seventh Sister.

"I am one of the Pleiades, and I came here to find out how you live your lives in sisterhood strong for peace, working for a universal family of all humanity, and to tell you of how my six sister stars and I live. Please, tell me about yourselves," asks Seventh Sister.

January 1, '83 * Dancing on the silos where cruise missiles are to be stored.

Slowly, the women tell Seventh Sister about their lives at the Common. Camping out near the base, cutting its fences and showing the military how secure its security really is, dancing on the missile silos, their nights around the camp fires talking and sometimes wondering what the stars were thinking about them. They tell Seventh Sister about following secret military convoys through the gates and through the night to leak the news to the press and keep the military's clandestine activities aimed towards death out in the open; at least, a little bit more so. They tell her of tracing a convoy through sharp thorns and mud, to be discovered by an equally muddy soldier on patrol just after they had seen the convoy's hiding place. (Hiro smiles broadly at this point, saying, "Our being discovered meant they had to find another hiding place, and go through what we had been through to track them once again.")

They told Seventh Sister how strange it seemed to them that land prices in Greenham Common had gone down since they had arrived. Having a peace camp in the area, apparently, is less lucrative to real estate people than having a military base in the area. Seventh Sister laughed at the grimaces Deb made imitating the realtors. The women said they had never heard anything so beautiful as the star's laughter. Seventh Sister was pleased at this and laughed again, from joy rather than hilarity. A laughter of a different quality and beauty filled the air.

The women listened attentively as Seventh Sister told about how curious she and the other six sisters had been about them, and then stopped as she saw a small tree, decorated with little paper gifts upon it, and stones and shells below it. "What's that?"

Isia went over to the baby pine tree and crouched. She spoke softly and slowly, and ended singing, and all of the women joined in. She said, "We had a sister Andy, 28 year old Mother of Toby, 2 ½, and Polly, 8, beloved wife of Niel. She strove for a Peaceful Life for them All. She Camped Here until Sunday 30th September, knowing on the 1st October she was to have a major cancer operation. She never recovered. We wish her to be remembered for her bravery and know that part of her is still with us All. Her ashes are buried beneath this tree. So far, the police have left it alone." She sang, and all the women joined in:

> "You can't kill the Spirit,
> She is like a mountain,
> Old and Strong,
> She still goes on..."

After several hours of sharing and laughing and crying and communing together, Seventh Sister said, "I must return now, with the night-fall, to my home. My six sisters are waiting for me. Thank you for the wonderful visit, and I'm glad I arrived here just in time to help you start that fire. Please help me return by putting a handful of water over me, each of you."

Each woman approached, carefully balancing a palmful of water over to the star. They spoke blessings to Seventh Sister as they dropped the water over her, and some of the women left their blessings unspoken. With the last handful of water, a mist started to rise around the star, and rose in a steamy cloud of light, higher and higher.

Seventh Sister is once again dim and blinking, as before. If you ask the women of Greenham Common, especially at the yellow gate, they'll tell you it's their sister, Seventh Sister, losing her concentration on glowing because she's exchanging the stories she learned on Earth from her Greenham sisters with her six star sisters.

*December 12, '82 * 30,000 women encircle the Greenham Common base to demonstrate their opposition to nuclear weapons, and commitment to peace.*

I am in the world to change the world.
-- Käthe Kollwitz

The Meditation Teacher and the Warrior

(Archan Po and Tan Ratanando, monks at the Buddhist monastery of Wot Suan Moke, in Suratthani Province, Thailand, recommended meditation as a way of gaining inner peace, as a step towards working for a true social peace. Archan Po explains that wars are always caused by people's uncontrolled desires, and can always be traced to these desires. If people had more control of themselves and their desires, attained through thoughtful insight, there would be much less war -- it would evaporate. Now, however, people find it easier to control monstrous weapons rather than gain control of their desires, to control themselves. Tan Ratanando told this story:)

There was once a meditation teacher who received a request for lessons in Vipassana meditation from a warrior. The warrior was given instruction in breath awareness, mindfulness, and effort. For several years, the warrior tried to meditate, but seemed to make no progress. The warrior came and told the meditation teacher, who said, "You are not putting in enough effort. Try harder."

The warrior left and tried harder for several years, and still made no progress. The teacher said that greater effort still was necessary. Again, the warrior put forth more effort into the meditation, and had to return with a similar tale of lack of progress after another few years of effort.

"Very well," said the teacher, "What do you like to do? What is something that you like a great deal?"

"Well, I like chess," responded the warrior.

"Good. Then we'll play a game of chess together," said the teacher, and prepared the board. "Whoever wins will cut off the head of the one who loses." They started to play.

At first, the warrior played normally. The reality of the game started to penetrate, however, and the warrior started to fear for the loss of the game, and the loss of his head. He started to panic, and make bad moves, and lose. Then he realized that he had to pay attention to the game, only, if he wanted to survive. He centered his concentration on the game, and threw away all his fears of losing the game, and threw away all fears of losing his life. He became the chess game. He started to win. Then, he realized that if he won, he would have to cut off the head of his meditation teacher. He didn't want to do this. As this thought entered his mind, he looked into the face of the teacher.

As he looked into the teacher's face, he saw no trace of fear, even though the teacher was perhaps close to death. He saw in the teacher's eyes that they had led many young people along the path of wisdom. He said to himself, "Who am I, who have done nothing but destroy throughout my life; who am I to take the life of this wise one?" When this thought entered his mind, he decided to lose the game, and started to make bad moves on purpose.

As soon as the warrior started losing the game purposely, the meditation teacher got up, turned the board over, upset the pieces, and said, "Now, you have truly won -- for at the moment that wisdom is born, compassion is born, also."

North East Germany, 1945
--Ursula Friedrichson

I was one of 20 German women who had been taken to a remote farm to wash the dirty laundry of Russian soldiers. We tried to sleep in piles of straw in the barn, when a thunderous knocking at the door shocked us from our rest. It could only mean "Rape!" I opened the huge door. Two Russian soldiers explained that I was to accompany them. I waved "Good-bye!" to my friends.

I was led through the snow to a small room. A young Russian soldier lay crying on the floor, his right foot bleeding from a rifle shot -- self-inflicted, obviously, so he would be sent home. But it meant he might be shot as a deserter. I found the shell, ordered hot water, cleaned the wound, and bandaged it -- I always carried a torn sheet under my coat, in case of emergency.

I tried to convince everybody that the shot had been accidental.

The poor youngster cried and cried, and I kissed him.

I was escorted back to my friends. When I opened the door, all my German women friends were kneeling on the cold stone floor -- praying for me.

In the grey morning, we were awakened by Russian soldiers banging at the door. Outside stood our open lorry with a row of packages with bread, food, and flour. I was retained by an officer. "Why did you try so hard to save the life of a doomed boy?" he asked, "We are your enemies."

"My nephew is at the Eastern front!" I answered, "the same age as that innocent kid!"

"I thank you with all my heart!" he said with tears in his eyes, "I am a father, too! Go home in peace!" and he kissed me.

Mother and Child

-- Käthe Kollwitz

The Samurai and the Monk

> --as told by Reuven Gold,
> who heard it from Ken Feit

A Samurai walks into a Zen monastery, big, strong, with fine samurai swords hanging from his belt. He walks up to the little monk eating and says, "Monk, teach me the difference between heaven and hell!"

The Monk puts down his food and looks at the Samurai. "I cannot," he begins calmly, "You are much too stupid."

The Samurai feels anger boiling in his belly, steel's cold taste between his teeth. He gives a grunt of rage and touches his sword.

"And besides that," continues the Monk, "you're ugly."

The Samurai gives a cry of rage, anger flaming up in his belly, the taste of the cold steel sword of anger between his teeth. He grabs a sword, and lifts it over his head, his arm trembling in rage.

The Monk says, "That is hell."

The Samurai realizes that with only a few words, the Monk has defeated his feelings of self-control, has driven him to the point of killing the Monk over a few words, has driven him to a raging anger. He realizes that the Monk had been teaching him with all beneficence within the harsh-sounding words. He slowly brings down the sword, tucks it into his belt, and bows his head in humility.

The Monk looks at the Samurai and says, "And that ... that is heaven."

The Poor Elephants of the Ueno Zoo

(Several people in Japan shared pieces of this story, since it touched them so strongly. This version comes, with the students' permission, from the Messages for Tomorrow, edited and published by the Kobe City University of Foreign Studies Student Body Association; and enriched with information from the heavily-researched play The Zoo Without an Elephant, performed by the Zenshin-Za Theater Company for Children, of Tokyo, Japan, and with their blessing.)

In the Ueno Zoo, the cherry blossoms are now at their best. Some are blown off suddenly by a gust of wind, and some are shining beautifully with the sunshine. Many people who want to view them have come to the zoo, which is very crowded. A cloud of dust is raised here and there.

In the square in front of a cage, two elephants are now performing their feats. With their long trunks waving skyward, they shake flags in the sun, or throw rings, and walk to and fro on a log. Their performance makes many spectators shout for joy. A little distant from that busy square, there is a tombstone. Few people become aware of it, but it is the tomb where the animals who were killed as part of the war effort from the zoo are buried.

One day, a man working in the zoo, and stroking this tombstone with deep emotion, told me the sad story of the elephants.

Now, there are three elephants in the zoo. Their names are Jampoh, India, and Menamu; but formerly, there were as well three elephants, named John, Tonky, and Wanly. At that time, Japan was at war with the U.S.A. The war was violent, and a lot of bombs were dropped on Tokyo like heavy rain, day after day, night after night. The military worried about what would happen if the bombs were dropped on the zoos. They conjectured that if the cages were broken and frightened beasts attacked people, it would be serious. They gave orders to zoo personnel to poison lions, tigers, leopards, bears, and big snakes. Despite the gentleness of the elephants, the military leaders decided to order the zoo to kill the three elephants, also.

The first elephant they had to kill was John, who was always naughty, and unmanageable. As John liked potatoes very much, I fed him poisoed potatoes, which were mixed in with other good potatoes. However, clever John threw them away as soon as he brought them to his mouth with his long trunk.

They decided to give an injection of poison to him. The big hypodermic needle which was normally used for horses was brought. When they attempted to inject the poison, however, all of the needles broke because of his tough skin. It didn't work.

The zoo personnel asked the military if they could shoot John, in order to make a quick end for the poor beast. The military argued that a bullet shot would frighten the people of the city. The zoo personnel were forced to stop feeding him, and, after thirteen days without food, John died.

Now it was Tonky's and Wanly's turns. Tonky and Wanly always stared with their pretty eyes and had kind hearts. For these reasons, the people working at the zoo felt sympathy for them and tried to rescue them. They contacted the Sendai Zoo in the Tohoku District, and found ready quarters for the elephants. The military complex, however, refused this possibility, saying that Tokyo was the capital, and should show courage to the other cities by allowing its elephants to be sacrificed for the war effort.

Days passed when they did not give food to the animals. Both Wanly and Tonky became thinner and thinner, and turned more low-spirited.

When they saw the tamer going his rounds, they stood unsteadily, and trumpeted in a thin voice , as if they were saying, "Would you feed us? We want something to eat."

In a few days, their eyes began to pop, like a ball, out of their faces which had become remarkably thin. The two elephants turned into sad and pitiful figures whose ears alone looked comparatively big.

The caretaker of the elephants had loved them like his own children so far, but he could do nothing except walk up and down before the cage and say, "Ah, what a pity! What a pity!"

Suddenly, Wanly and Tonky staggered to their feet and stepped toward their caretaker. They began to perform one of their tricks, leaning on each other's tired back. They stood on their hind legs, and they sat up... They lifted up their trunks cheerfully, and showed the trainer and the nearby zoo visitors stunts with all the strength of their skinny, tired bodies.

They thought that if they did stunts, they could get food. Both Tonky and Wanly tried to give it their best in spite of their tottering steps. The elephant's caretaker could not watch them with a straight face any longer. "Oh, Wanly! Oh, Tonky!" -- he rushed into the cage with some food. He returned with more water and food, and threw these at the elephants' feet. "Hey, eat and eat, drink and drink," he said, clinging to the leg of the elephant. All the zoo employees pretended not to see this scene. The zoo director also bit his lips and only watched over the desk.

The zoo employees had been told by the military that the animals should not be fed, that the elephants should not receive water, that they must kill the elephants whether they liked it or not. However, everyone thought that feeding the elephants secretly would cause them to live until the end of the war, and everyone prayed to God for that. Zoo employees and private citizens combed the city's trash bins for food for the elephants. But, at last, both Tonky and Wanly could not move any more. All they could do was to look up at the clouds floating in the sky, lying still hopelessly on the ground.

The elephant caretaker was too heart-broken to visit them. Other people also could not endure to see them and stayed far away from the elephant cage. At last, Wanly, about two weeks later, and Tonky, about three weeks later, died, each leaning against the iron cage, and holding high its thin trunk. The cry went up, "They're dead! They're dead!"

The elephant caretaker rushed into the zoo office crying like a mad man. He struck the desk with his fist, and then burst into weeping.

Workers of the zoo rushed to the elephant cage and entered it as if they were rolling. They clung to the elephants. They shook their bodies. All of the people began to cry bitterly. Above, the skies of Tokyo were roaring with enemy bombers. All threw themselves onto the bodies of the elephants and held on to them while raising their clenched fists and calling out, "Terminate the war!" "Please put an end to war! Please!"

As the people looked at the bodies of the elephants, they could see that there wasn't even a drop of water left in those stomachs as big as tubs. Now the elephants are sleeping quietly, eternally under the grave marker in the Ueno Zoo.

The old elephant caretaker told me the story with tears in his eyes. For a long time afterward, we stood silently beside the stone grave covered with the petals of cherry blossoms.

The Little Fishes and Chiko in the Sea

(The RNC Theater Company of Takamatsu, Japan, felt a need to express, artistically, the love of life they experience, and a gentle, firm message to children that the disaster of Hiroshima will never be replicated if they, also, work for peace. Playwright Ryozo Yagi came up with a play, <u>Ototo to Chiko no Umi</u>, whose story is told below, with sincere appreciation to Fusako Kurahara and Motoko Hori Foster for translating story and song for this book, and to RNC for permission to retell the story.)

Chiko is laughing and playing alone near the seashore, when she hears her friends coming down the road. She turns to them, and they soon argue and fight over some trifle. Her friends leave. Chiko feels misunderstood, and jumps into the sea.

As she jumps into Hiroshima Bay, Chiko sees the little fish of varied colors around her, and they guide her to the Old Wise Woman Fish. Chiko explains what she has done, and the Old Wise Woman Fish tells the little fish to take Chiko back quickly, for this child should live.

The little fish start to push Chiko, who does <u>not</u> understand why the Old Wise Woman Fish said that she should leave so quickly. When the little fish see that Chiko will not be persuaded, they swim toward a small dent in the Hiroshima Bay depths. In this dent are several small skulls, singing,

The Lullaby of the Child's Skulls

Kalarin, kalarin, the sound of the skulls.
I remember the sad day and crying --
My tear in the dark socket.
How terrible that day was --
I couldn't even cry out
with my mouth, or with my tongue.
I remember how happy I had been --
but now I cannot express my laughter
with my cold, chilly face.
My smile is gone.
Kalarin, kalarin, the sound of the skulls.

The little fish tell Chiko that this is the place where they had brought the skulls of the children who had been burned badly in Hiroshima, on the day of the atom bomb, and had run to the river, and died there. The river brought their bodies to this bay, and the little fish tell Chiko that they have gathered the skulls here so they could pray over them, in their own manner as fish. Also, they were all children who wanted to live, but had been forced to die. They want Chiko to understand how important it is to live life intensely and peacefully. They tell Chiko that her prayers, and the prayers and actions of other human children, and adults, would probably be stronger for these children whose skulls they saw before them, than the fishes' prayers.

Chiko understands the little fish and gathers up the skulls, promising to take them to a place where they will receive respect. She thanks the little fish, and walks back out of Hiroshima Bay to live life intensely and peacefully.

Peace through Aloha

(In Hawaii, there is a kahuna, a sage, who is well-known for her wisdom and strength of conviction. She has been a vocal element in her community for a retention of the beauty and depth of traditional hawaii culture. When asked to give her ideas on how world peace could be obtained, Pilahi Paki gave this poem/blessing. To her, "Aloha" retains the traditional hawaii meaning of kindness, unity, humility, and patient perseverance.)

He Pule

My Prayer

There is promise in Aloha
For each day the sun rises,
Hope in Aloha
In each new day that begins,
Sunlight in Aloha
In work that we must do,
Grace in Aloha
To meet all of life's problems,
Help in Aloha
For all those difficult moments,
Mercy and compassion in Aloha
for the trials we face,
Love in Aloha
Boundless and forever,
Peace in Aloha
Quiet and true
When we understand
There is a God of Aloha
Walking life's pathways with us.

Pilahi Paki

Song for a Russian Mother

-- Holly Gwinn Graham

I do not know your name, or how you look,
Or what you might be wearing every day,
And yet we might be friends,
If there were not an ocean and such hatred in the way.
Oh, Russian mother, so far across the sea,
And in our children's eyes
We see their promise
While their laughter echoes on the wind --
Another generation with its own dreams to begin:
The sound of children running home to suppertime,
The final bedtime story cuddled by the fireside,
The innocence of slumber on each face,
The future of the family and all the human race
Here in our hands --
Oh, I would get to know you, and
To understand the things you want of life,
And how you make them true.
Oh, there is much that I would learn from you -
A recipe, a song or three, your favorite country walk,
Perhaps in time, the language shared,
We'd sip strong tea and talk about our motherhood,
About our dreams and plans, about our children's lives,
About these crazy men who run our world around!

How did we ever get so lost?
How are we ever to be found?
In family, in peace and simple living,
In sisterhood, in loving and forgiving.

I do not know your name, or how you look,
Or what you might be wearing every day,
And yet we will be friends --
Oh, let there be no ocean and no hatred in the way.
Oh, Russian mother, across the sea so far,
I can't help thinking how very similar we are.

© 1982 by Holly Graham &
    Harbor Seal Publishing
All rights reserved
Used by Permission

*Traditional Paper Cut-out
Museum of Ethnography
Torun, Poland*

We Shall Bring Forth New Life

-- Sadako Kurihara

(translated by Wayne Lammers)

It was night in the basement of a broken building.
Victims of the atomic bomb
Crowded into the candleless darkness,
Filling the room to overflowing --
The smell of fresh blood, the stench of death,
The stuffiness of human sweat, the writhing moans --
When, out of the darkness, came a wondrous voice.
"Oh, the baby's coming!" it said.
In the basement turned to living hell
A young woman had gone into labor!
The others forgot their own pain in their concern:
What could they do for her, having not even a match
To bring light to the darkness?
Then! Another voice: "I am a midwife.
I can help her with the baby."
It was a woman who had been moaning in pain
only moments before.
And so, a new life was born
In the darkness of that living hell.
And so, the midwife died before dawn.
We shall bring forth new life!
We shall bring forth new life!
Even to our death.

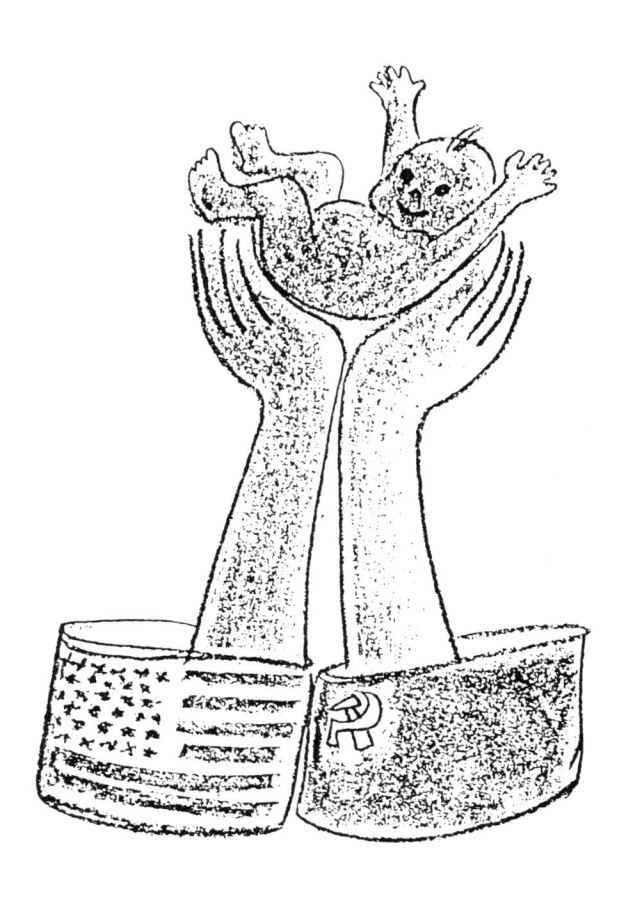

Family Promise

-- Holly Near, lyrics

Holly Near & Jeff Langley, music

Finally a baby born in the spring time
Then helping us all face a death in our lives
Your mother and your grandma and your aunts so proud and grateful
Your father and you are now the men in our lives.

But outside the shelter, the war claims the children
That you might grow up to be friends with one day
And what of the water, the air and the desert
We make a family promise on your first birthday
While we're alive in this world
We will try to disarm every nuclear nation
An everyday gift to the world
A gift to ourselves, while we're alive

Amazed by the details we watch you for hours
Just like our dad did, you make us all smile
Such inspiration for facing the future
Demanding survival, your fist still so small
While we're alive in this world
We will try to disarm every nation
An everyday gift to the world
A gift to ourselves, while we're alive.

© 1982 by Hereford Music
All rights reserved
Used by Permission

I Come and Stand ...
            -- Nazim Hikmet

I come and stand at every door
But no one hears my silent tread.
I knock, but yet remain unseen
For I am dead, for I am dead.

I'm only seven though I died
In Hiroshima long ago.
I'm seven now as I was then --
When children die, they do not grow.

My hair was scorched by swirling fire,
My eyes grew dim, my eyes grew blind --
Death came and turned my bones to dust
That was scattered by the wind.

I need no fruit, I need no rice,
I need no sweets or even bread;
I ask for nothing for myself
For I am dead, for I am dead.

All I ask is that for peace
You strive today, you strive today
So that the children of the world
Can live and grow and laugh and play.

I come and stand at every door
But no one hears my silent tread.
I knock, but yet remain unseen
For I am dead, for I am dead.

*If we could read the secret history of our "enemies",
we should find in each one's life
sorrow and suffering enough to disarm all hostility.*

            -- Longfellow

Okori Jizo
(The Angry Buddha)
--Yuko Yamaguchi

On the day that Hiroshima was bombed, a jizo, a stone statue of Buddha, was buried in rubble up to its neck. The jizo watched the people running back and forth, covered with burns, and filled with terror. A girl with burns all over her back was stumbling down the road, asking for water from each passerby, but no one had the ability to listen since they were all filled with their own pain, thirst, and fear.

She fell in front of the jizo, and said, "Water, please give me some water! Omizu, kudasai! Water!"

The jizo's stone heart was touched by the suffering of the girl. The jizo's stone heart had more compassion in it than those of the people who could drop such a bomb on other people, and the jizo wanted to help her. Up until then, its stone face was smiling, but, calling on every reserve of strength and compassion, the jizo started to shed tears.

After quenching her thirst with these tears of the jizo's compassion, the girl died. The jizo was so angered by the heartlessness of these people who drop such a bomb on other people, and was so saddened by the death of the young girl, that the jizo's head fell from his shoulders, rolled, and cradled against the head of the girl.

The White Ship on the Dream Island

(Akio Araki cooperated as the playwright who would work with Kyogei Puppet Theater of Kyoto to create a play on the theme of peace. This play features the tuna fishing boat Dogai Fukuryu Maru (or "Fifth Lucky Dragon") as the main character of the play. Ms. Fusako Kurahara translates as Mr. Araki and the Kyogei Puppet Theater retell the boat's story from the viewpoint of the historical character Dogai Fukuryu Maru.)

On the day that all of this began for me, we were off the Bikini Islands on a beautiful March day, having been out for a few weeks already, and my hold was full of tuna. Suddenly, a strange rain of ashes came down on us, and we all marveled at what this stuff might be, not taking it very seriously. But from the next day, some of the crew members started to get headaches, and soon, black splotches started to come out on their skin. They started to wonder amongst themselves about the significance of the strange black rain, and decided to turn me back to Yaizu, our home port in Japan.

At Yaizu, the crew members were taken immediately to hospitals. My tuna catch was, by some administrative error, distributed to some extent before someone noticed the oversight, and stopped the distribution until a radioactivity check could be taken. This proved the fish were poisonous, and had to be thrown away. It was also discovered that the weird black rain had been caused by a hydrogen-bomb test by the USA some miles away from us on that March day. I found out later that one of the crew members, Aikichi Kuboyama by name, died in September of the same year, 1954. His dying words urged people to stop creating such cruelty to other people by stopping the testing and creation of such bombs.

...RVICES IN CONJUNCTION WITH THE GREEN ROOM IN

FLOATING EAGLE FEATHER

Now, for awhile, I thought I had been forgotten, but, when the tuna catch was eliminated, they wondered about me, and decided to tow me out to a trashpile. The police ship took me there, but I succeeded in escaping. Iron, a tugboat friend, aided me, but we were soon caught. Iron ran aground and I was pulled back to the trash heap.

My life became quite dull for some time, until a mouse happened onto my deck, and I called out to her, and we started to talk. She called to a seagull nearby, and introduced me. The seagull asked me to tell them how I'd gotten to the "Dream Island", which was the name of the trash heap.

I told them about the USA H-Bomb test, the strange rain of ash, the poisoned tuna, and radio operator Aikichi's death. I told the mouse and seagull about my unsuccessful escape, and my friend Iron's fate. I sighed and said, "And now, here I am, on Yumenoshima, the Dream Island, with no one to whom I could tell my tale until you two good friends came along."

The mouse and the seagull thought together about how they could help me, and began looking for someone who might be interested in saving me. They fly close to a ship's carpenter and tell him the story of the ship they'd found, and ask him if he'd like to help the Fukuryu Maru.

The ship's carpenter is overjoyed to hear these words! He says that now, he is old, "But some time ago, when I had finished my apprenticeship, I decided to build a small ship. She turned out beautifully, and I always felt like that first ship was a daughter to me. I've been looking for her for awhile now, and I think Fukuryu Maru is the ship I'm seeking!"

My friends started to bring the carpenter to me at Dream Island, and I wondered who this old man approaching me could be. As he came towards me, I could hear him saying, "And then, I was called for a soldier, and I didn't like the war. I only wanted to get back home and look for my daughter, my first ship, Fukuryu Maru." I was very happy to hear those words -- as happy as wood and joist can be, I was.

Well, he started to fix me up, but I had been on Dream Island decaying for too long. I wasn't seaworthy in spite of his efforts, with all the help that Mouse and Seagull were able to give.

Listen, my friends! I am a hibakusha, an atomic bomb victim. I, and the 23 members of my crew, were "peacetime" bomb victims, and reminded the people of Japan and of the world of the need to work for peace with greater effort. Perhaps, if I tell my sad story, people will not let this happen to any other boats or crews. If you want to talk to me, come visit me at Yumenoshima, Dream Island, just on the edge of Tokyo. I am too old to move anyplace on my own anymore. I am here! I am here!

Fighting Leads to Losses

-- a Jataka story from India
told by Cathy Spagnoli

A jackal who was newly-married lived near a riverbank. One day, his bride asked him for a meal of fish. He promised to bring some, even though he did not know how to swim. He crept up quietly to the river and watched two otters who were struggling with a huge fish they had caught. After killing the fish, the two began to fight about how to divide it.

"I saw it first, so I should have the largest portion," said one.

"But I saved you when you almost drowned while catching the fish," argued the other.

They continued to fight until the jackal walked up to them and offered to settle the argument. The otters agreed to abide by his decision. He cut the fish in three pieces. To one otter, he gave the head, and to the other, the tail. "The middle," he said, "goes to the judge."

He walked away happily, saying, "Fighting always leads to losses."

The Frogs and the Bulls

-- Aesop

A frog one day, sitting at the edge of the pond, saw two bulls fighting in a meadow. He cried out to a companion, "Look at that dreadful fight! What will become of us?"

"Do not frighten yourself," replied the other, "How can their quarrels affect us? They are quite different from us in every way."

"Perhaps their lives are different from ours," said the first frog, "But, as one of them will certainly get the better of the other, the one who is beaten will take refuge here in the marshes, and perhaps tread on some of us. You see, therefore, we are more concerned with their quarrel than you think."

MORAL:

When the rich quarrel, the poor are usually the greatest sufferers.

The Snipe and the Mussel

A mussel was opening its shell to bask in the sun when a snipe pecked at it. The mussel clamped down on the bird's beak and help it fast.

"If it doesn't rain today or tomorrow," said the snipe, "there will be a dead mussel lying here."

"If you can't pry loose today or tomorrow," retorted the mussel, "there will be a dead snipe here, too."

As neither of them would give way, a passing fisherman caught them both.

-- Peng Tong
(from Warring States Anecdotes, compiled by Liu Xang.)

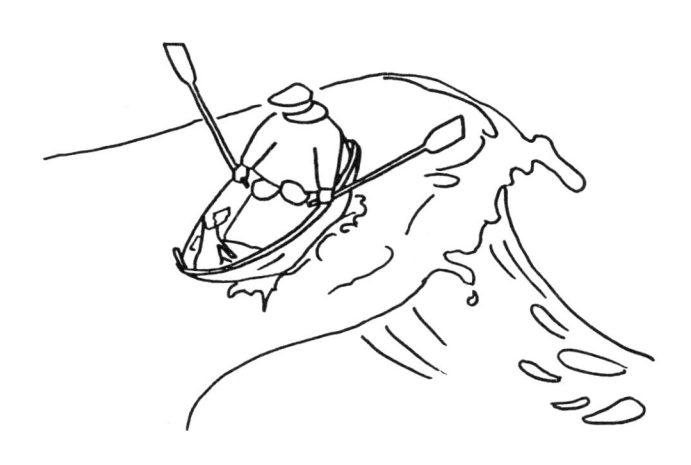

Alexander and the Pirates

--Gesta Romanorum

("Exploits of the Romans")

For a long time, a mariner named Diomedes sailed the seas in a galley, attacking the shipping, plundering the cargoes, and sinking the vessels. At last he was captured and brought before Alexander the Great, who asked angrily how he dared to trouble the seas as he had done.

"Sire," said he, "ask rather how you dare to trouble the earth. I am master of only a single galley, and do but little harm, while you are master of great fleets, and carry desolation and war. Yet I am called a robber, and you are a king and conqueror. Did fortune but change, and I became more successful, while you became less successful, our positions might be reversed."

This argument so struck the king that he made the pirate a wealthy prince, on condition that he give up making his living as a robber, and become honest.

Life is a Cosmic Bivouac

-- Evi Seidman

Life is a cosmic bivouac. You get dropped off in the middle of the night, blindfolded, with no equipment or supplies, no maps, no information, nothing to wear, you don't know the language, you don't know anyone there -- you parachute down. This phase is called Project Birth.

Your mission, should you choose to accept it, is simply to complete the cycle and return to home base. This phase is called Operation Survival.

You will be expected to negotiate a difficult obstacle course. Half the people you meet along the way have instructions to secretly deter, detain, or confuse you. Several will offer you cigarettes and glazed donuts. Fortunately, the other half have instructions to secretly assist you: children, skid-row derelicts, grocery store clerks. When you least expect it, they toss you a line: return your lost wallet to you (with the cash still in it) or let you make a left hand turn from the right lane (with a smile, even!) There are clues everywhere.

Operation Survival is estimated to take somewhere between 65 and 90 years to complete. However, certain candidates are dropped from the roles earlier in the program due to genetic slip-ups, highway collisions, asbestos in their drinking water, radioactive chicken pot pies --- any number of unfortunate accidents.

And of course, occasionally a few simply resign from the program by leaping from tall buildings without a single bounce. But, this is to be discouraged. It is a distinct disadvantage to resign from the program in that the enrollee must still repeat parachuting and Project Birth until you get it right. This is a volunteer program only to a degree.

Operation Survival is successfully completed at the natural end of the obstacle course, which generally happens around the time of old age.

The third phase of Cosmic Bivouac is Project Death. (Notice that I did not say the "Final Phase". There is no need for this subject to be grim.) Project Death is the least understood part of the program. Though it's simple, really. It's like a mud puddle drying up in the sun after a rain. The soil stays on the earth but the water is taken up into the clouds as vapor. But people are funny. They don't mind at all being the rain, but they don't want to have to experience evaporation. And they don't want to be lost up in the clouds.

So if dying is drying up and borning is raining, what is life? Life must be a river. But what is the meaning of the river of life?

Well, we each cross that bridge when we come to it.

Military intelligence is a contradiction in terms.
-- Groucho Marx

Why We Oppose Votes for Men

1.

Because man's place is in the army.

2.

Because no really manly man wants to settle any question otherwise than by fighting about it.

3.

Because if men should adopt peaceable methods, women will no longer look up to them.

4.

Because men will lose their charm if they step out of their natural sphere and interest themselves in other matters than feats of arms, uniforms, and drums.

5.

Because men are too emotional to vote. Their conduct at baseball games and political conventions shows this, while their innate tendency to appeal to force renders them particularly unfit for the task of government.

-- Alice Duer Miller

We Hate to See Them Go
-- Malvina Reynolds

Last night, I had a lovely dream,
I saw a big parade with ticker tape galore,
And men were marching there the like I'd never seen before.

Oh, the bankers and the diplomats are going in the Army,
Oh, happy day, I'd give my pay to see them on parade.
Their paunches at attention and their striped pants at ease.
They've gotten patriotic and they're going overseas.
We'll have to do the best we can and bravely carry on,
So we'll just keep the laddies here to manage while they're gone.
Oh, oh, we hate to see them go,
The gentlemen of distinction in the Army.

The bankers and the diplomats are going in the Army,
It seemed too bad to keep them from the wars they love to plan,
We're all of us contented that they'll fight a dandy war,
They don't need propaganda, they know what they're fighting for.
They'll march away with dignity and in the best of form,
And we'll just keep the laddies here to keep the lassies warm.
Oh, oh, we hate to see them go,
The gentlemen of distinction in the Army.

The bankers and the diplomats are going in the Army,
We're going to make things easier 'cause it's all so new and strange--
We'll give them silver shovels when they have to dig a hole,
And they can sing in harmony when answering the roll,
They'll eat their old K-rations from a hand-embroidered box,
And when they die, we'll bring them home, and bury them in Fort Knox.
Oh, oh, we hate to see them go,
The gentlemen of distinction in the Army.

© 1959 by Schroder Music Co. (ASCAP)
All rights reserved.
Used by Permission.

When God wants to chastise nations,
God sends them warriors whose
only greatness is their weapons,
orators whose only greatness
is the length of their speeches,
and bankers whose only greatness
is the depth of their pockets.

— Anonymous

War Preparers Anonymous

(From a speech given by Kurt Vonnegut at the 92nd Street YM/YWHA in New York City, and printed in The Nation, January 7, '84, as "Weapons Junkies: the Worst Addiction of Them All.)

What has been America's most nurturing contribution to the culture of this planet so far? Many would say jazz. I, who love jazz, will say this instead: Alcoholics Anonymous.

I am not an alcoholic. If I were, I would go before the nearest A A meeting and say,"My name is Kurt Vonnegut. I am an alcoholic." God willing, that might be my first step down the long, hard road back to sobriety.

The AA scheme, which requires a confession like that, is the first to have any measurable success in dealing with the tendency of some human beings, perhaps 10 percent of any population, to become addicted to substances that give them brief spasms of pleasure but in the long term transmute their lives and the lives of those around them to ultimate ghastliness.

The AA scheme, which, again, can work only if the addicts regularly admit that this or that chemical is poisonous to them, is now proving its effectiveness with compulsive gamblers, who are not dependent on chemicals from a distillery or a pharmaceutical laboratory. This is no paradox. Gamblers, in effect, manufacture their own dangerous substances. God help them, they produce chemicals that elate them whenever they place a bet on simply anything.

If I were a compulsive gambler, which I am not, I would be well advised to stand up before the nearest meeting of Gamblers Anonymous and declare, "My name is Kurt Vonnegut. I am a compulsive gambler."

Whether I was standing before a meeting of Gamblers Anonymous or Alcoholics Anonymous, I would be encouraged to testify as to how the chemicals I had generated within myself, or swallowed had alienated my friends and relatives, cost me jobs and houses, and deprived me of my last shred of self-respect.

I now wish to call attention to another form of addiction, which has not been previously identified. It is more like gambling than drinking, since the people afflicted are ravenous for situations that will cause their bodies to release exciting chemicals into their bloodstreams. I am persuaded that there are among us people who are tragically hooked on preparations for war.

Tell people with that disease that war is coming and we have to get ready for it, and for a few minutes there they will be as happy as a drunk with his martini breakfast or a compulsive gambler with his paycheck bet on the Super Bowl.

Let us recognize how sick such people are. From now on, when a national leader, or even just a neighbor, starts talking about some new weapons system that is going to cost us a mere $29 billion, we should speak up. We should say something on the order of, "Honest to God, I couldn't be sorrier for you if I'd seen you wash down a fistful of black beauties with a pint of Southern Comfort."

I mean it. I am not joking. Compulsive preparers for World War III, in this country or any other, are as tragically and repulsively addicted as any stockbroker passed out with his head in a toilet in the Port Authority bus terminal.

For an alcoholic to experience a little joy, he needs maybe three ounces of grain alcohol. Alcoholics, when they are close to hitting bottom, customarily can't hold much alcohol.

If we know a compulsive gambler who is dead broke, we can probably make him happy with a dollar to bet on who can spit farther than someone else.

For us to give a compulsive war-preparer a fleeting moment of happiness, we may have to buy him three Trident submarines and a hundred intercontinental ballistic missiles mounted on choo-choo trains.

If Western Civilization were a person--

If Western Civilization, which blankets the world now, as far as I can tell, were a person--

If Western Civilization, which surely now includes the Soviet Union and China and India and Pakistan and on and on, were a person--

If Western Civilization were a person, we would be directing it to the nearest meeting of War Preparers Anonymous. We would be telling it to stand up before the meeting and say, "My name is Western Civilization. I am a compulsive war-preparer. I have lost everything I ever cared about. I should have come here long ago. I first hit bottom in World War I."

Western Civilization cannot be represented by a single person, of course, but a single explanation for the catastrophic course it has followed during this bloody century is possible. We the people, because of our ignorance of the disease, have again and again entrusted power to people we did not know were sickies.

And let us not mock them now, any more than we would mock someone with syphilis or smallpox or leprosy or yaws or typhoid fever or any of the other diseases to which the flesh is heir. All we have to do is to separate them from the levers of power, I think.

And then what?

Western Civilization's long, hard trip back to sobriety might begin.

MESSIAH ARRIVES!
(Purim, 1979; Adar, 5739)

(Exclusive to Not the Jewish Press) -- In what has to be the greatest event since the splitting of the Red Sea, our Israeli correspondents have just learned that the Messiah has finally arrived. After many false alarms and a few hoaxes over the years, this time, we are sure.

Mr. Mashiach Ben David had to fight unusually heavy rush-hour traffic, including a near-fatal accident with a bus en route to the Holy City. A final burst from his donkey brought the Messiah triumphantly through the gates of Jerusalem, where an enthusiastic crowd gave the Messiah a tumultuous welcome.

Advance public relations had arrived in Jerusalem so that Messiah's appearance was not totally unexpected. Representatives from a multitude of Israeli political parties were on hand to win favor in the eyes of the Messiah.

World reaction to the Messiah has been mixed. Mashiach's proposed trip to New York City has sparked much enthusiasm and generated great interest in the Big Apple. The purpose of this messianic visit is to attempt to unite the warring factors of the Jewish community in preparation for their forthcoming aliyah.

In the meantime, preparations in Israel are in full swing. The Ministry of Absorption has already started outlining its plan for the mass resurrection. Thousands of families are anxiously awaiting reunions with their ancestors, as well as the revelation of old family recipes. We have also learned that the Hebrew Union Prayerbook will be undergoing a massive overhaul. Finally, plans for world-wide peace continue as armament factories begin their conversion to plowshare production.

The Monster ~~~ Lawrence Island
-- a Siberian Yupik Inuit tale

(In ~~~~~~~ of peace, there is a need for examples of bravery and fear-~~~~ness. Mahatma Gandhi, Dorothy Day, Sadako Kurihara, and Käthe Kollwitz are excellent examples, but we need someone who is closer. One group of people have not yet learned the meaning of fear, are outspoken about their opinions, and are to be found everywhere. This group -- the children -- can teach us lessons of creativity, fearlessness, spontaneity and forgiveness which will help us to defeat that monster of war: nuclear weapons, and nuclear power.

Children do learn fears with which they must come to grips, and a good monster story is an excellent opportunity to do this. A child can bundle up their unnamed fears into the monster, and defeat these fears with the defeat of the monster. It is recommended, for this reason, that this story be told all the way through to a child, in order to respect this psychological magic.

This story was told by a woman who lives in Anchorage, Alaska whose name is Grace Cross Antoghame Akumelingekuk. She was born on St. Lawrence Island, and has the blood and stories of the Siberian Yupik Inuit people flowing through the little rivers and great streams of her body. One of the most beautiful stories she tells is the story of her name. Grace Cross is her legal name that she signs to papers; Antoghame Akumelingekuk are spirit names, her power names -- one is ugly, the other is beautiful. She explains that her people, the Siberian Yupik Inuit of St. Lawrence Island, believe that we have two mothers: a physical mother who holds us in her arms while we are alive; and a spirit mother, who can hardly wait for us to die so that she can hold us in her spirit arms. This is a comforting idea, that when we die, our spirit mother is waiting to hold us close to her spirit self. However, this does mean that there is a friendly competition between the physical mother and the spirit mother: the physical mother wants you to stay alive and in your body; the spirit mother wants you to die and leave your body. The physical mother, when she sees the child getting sick, says, "Oh, the spirit mother is trying to pull the child's soul from the body."

She has various ways of helping the child's spirit to stay in the body. One of these is by giving the child an ugly name. Her name, for example, is "Antoghame", which means, "She who walks in the sewers." Imagine your spirit mother coming up to you and saying, "Oh, what a beautiful child! I'm going to take you away right now -- you're going to die. What's your name, dear?" And you respond, "Antoghame -- She who walks in the sewers", and she will say, your spirit mother will say, "Oh, never mind, I'll come for you later. Good-bye!"

Her other name, her beautiful name, is "Akumelingekuk", which means, "She who never sits down" -- she's always working hard to serve others, to take care of others, feeding animals, watering plants, teaching children. Here, then, is a Siberian Yupik Inuit story, told by Grace Cross Antoghame Akumelingekuk:)

The Monster of St. Lawrence Island

There were once many people who lived in many villages on St. Lawrence Island. They were very happy -- as happy as most people are -- except for one thing: there was a monster who would come to St. Lawrence Island and eat the people.

This monster was awful! It was as big as a whale -- and you know how big a whale is -- but it didn't have a whale's body. It had a human body, a body like yours or mine, but it was as big as a whale. It had a body, legs, and arms like ours, but, instead of having hands like ours, it had hands with seals instead of fingers. A black, a brown, a red, a white, a yellow seal -- each of its fingers was a different kind of seal. It had legs like ours, but, instead of having feet like ours, it had another pair of hands. These hands also had seals instead of fingers, so it walked on all fours. It had a head like ours, with eyes where our eyes are, but, of course, its eyes were as big as plates. It had a nose where our nose is, but, instead of having a mouth where our mouth is, it had a great, big lump on the front of its face. And, instead of having a mouth on the front of the lump, it had a great, big mouth across its lower back.

When it would come out of the water, it would make an awful sound, something like this, "Lub, lub, lub", and the people of the village would say, "Oh, no, here comes the monster! We'll all have to run again!" They would all start to run, but, always, the monster would catch one of the people, and then, (and this was the worst thing about the monster), it played with its food. It caught the person, brought the person up close to itself, and let the person go. The person would run away screaming and yelling. The monster would catch the person again, bring the person close, let the person go, the person would run away screaming and yelling, the monster would catch the person again. The monster would do this over and over until the person would be puffing and grunting for breath, at which time the monster would pick up the person, put the person down, smash the person with that great, big lump on the front of its face, and put that person into its mouth, and chew the person up. (At this point, the story-teller should bend forward and backward at the waist to show the action of the monster's jaws in their peculiar location in the lower back.) The monster was awful!

The people tried everything to get rid of the monster -- they threw stones and sticks, spears and arrows, but they all just disappeared as soon as they touched the monster's skin. One village decided to try fire. They gathered great heaps of dry sticks, and put flaming tips on their spears and arrows. When they heard the monster coming, "Lub, lub, lub," they tried their trick. They lit the bonfires, lit the flaming tips of the spears and arrows, pushed the bonfires towards the monster, and launched the flaming spears and arrows towards the monster. But their trick backfired: the monster took the fire in through its skin, and now it was even worse! It burned many of the houses as it went through the village, captured a person, brought the person up close, let the person go, the person ran away screaming and yelling, the monster caught the person, over and over, until the person was grunting and puffing for breath, at which time the monster picked the person up, held the person, breathed on the person, -- P U F F ! -- roasted the person, put the person into its mouth, and chewed the person up, (and, again, the storyteller flexes at the waist.) The monster was awful, and no one ever tried fire again.

Now, in one of these villages there lived a couple who had never had any children. They wanted very much to have a child, and were very happy when they finally had one. And the whole village was very happy because the monster didn't come to their village for three years after the baby was born. Oh, it kept coming to other villages of St. Lawrence Island, but, for some reason, it didn't come to this village, until, one day soon after the baby was three years old, they heard the monster, "Lub, lub, lub." The people said, "Well, at least we have had three years of happiness, but now, we will have to run again."

Everyone started to run. The woman grabbed the baby, the man grabbed a spear. The woman was so afraid of her own life, as well as that of the child, that she ran faster than her husband, she ran faster than any of the other villagers. She ran until she came to the front of the group of villagers, and far outdistanced all of them -- holding the baby the whole time! She ran until she came to the bottom of the mountain, and started to run up the mountain. When she was about halfway up the mountain, she decided to see how close the monster was, and how close the rest of her people were. She turned around to look, and, as she turned around, her foot slipped on a piece of loose gravel, her arms flew open as she fell back. The baby flew up, landed on the soft grass, rolled down the mountain, and stopped ... right ... in front ... of the monster!

The monster was very confused. Usually, people were much bigger. This was a very small person. Not only that, but people, who were usually much bigger, usually ran away, screaming and yelling. This person had come towards the monster. Not only that, but the baby had rather enjoyed the roll down the mountain and was laughing. The monster was confused: usually, people were bigger, ran away screaming and yelling; this person was small, had approached the monster, and was laughing. The monster thought, "Maybe this thing isn't really a person, maybe it's a trick, maybe it's poison. I'd better check this out." (Now, even though the monster had eyes as big as plates, it couldn't see very well. It bent down.)
...

"One arm, two arms. Just like a person."
"One leg, two legs. Just like a person."
The monster was still confused. It touched the baby's stomach.
"Kee, kee, kee, kee!" The baby giggled at the tickling seal-finger.
The monster had never heard such a sound before. It was still confused. It decided, "I'll see if it smells like a person." The monster picked up the baby, smelled the baby. "Uuuuugh!" The monster had never smelled anything so awful; surely no human being could smell this bad! The monster put the baby down. It decided to look again, very closely, to see if this thing really looked like a human. (Now, even though the monster had eyes as big as plates, it couldn't see very well.) It bent down.

The baby could be bothered less with the monster. The baby was playing in the sand, in the dirt, and took two handfuls of sand and threw them into the air -- right into the monster's eyes.

"Aaaaah!" the monster called through its mouth on its back. You can imagine how much it hurt the monster to have two handfuls of sand thrown right into its eyes -- you know how much it hurts to get a little speck of something in your eye. And its eyes were as big as plates! "Aaaaah!" it called through its mouth on its back.

The monster decided, "I don't care what this thing is! I'm going to chew it up until it's a liquid, and then I'm going to swallow it!" The monster picked up the baby, and was just about to drop the baby into its mouth, when the man came up and threw the spear right into the monster's mouth. The monster disappeared in a gust of wind, which blew the man over backwards, and the baby landed where the monster had been standing.

The man came up and hugged the baby. The woman came up and hugged the baby. He said, "What happened? What happened? I couldn't see!" She said, "When you threw the spear, it fell into the monster's mouth, the monster disappeared in a gust of wind, which blew you over backwards, and that's why you didn't see what happened. And the baby landed where the monster was standing."

Well, they went home with the baby between them, and they were all very happy, all the people of that baby's village, and all of the people of St. Lawrence Island, were very happy, since the monster disappeared that day somehow, even though nobody knows exactly how. And if you don't believe my story, you can go to St. Lawrence Island, and you can look as long as you want, but you won't find that monster, and that proves my story is true. And the baby?

The baby grew up to be a very happy adult.

"The Earth is Our Mother"
-- Karl Jadrnicek

The Paint Box
-- Tali Shurek, a child
(given by Cathy Spagnoli)

I have a paint box
with colors shining with delight;
I have a paint box
with colors warm and cool and bright:
I have no red
for blood and wounds,
I have no black
for an orphaned child,
I have no white
for the face of the dead,
I have no yellow
for burning sands.

I have orange
for joy and life,
I have blue
for bright, clear skies,
I have green
for buds and blooms,
I have pink
for dreams and rest.
I sat down and painted
Peace.

Why the Baby Says, "Goo - Goo"
--a Penobscot tale

(This story was told to the editor by several people in different ways. In one version, Nanabozo, the Spirit-Trickster of the Algonquin peoples, challenges anyone to a medicine fight. An old woman approaches him with a baby in her arms, and says the baby would win any medicine fight. "What! I can do anything that baby can do!" says Nanabozo. The old woman laughs and puts the baby on the ground. The baby is soon sucking a big toe. Nanabozo tries to do this, and admits defeat. This version was told to me by a friend, Jiiva Kala, whose laughing, joyous behavior whenever she was with the children showed her strong conviction that life, and its children, would always emerge victorious.)

There was once a great Penobscot chief who had done everything, seen everything, was very, very proud. As he was walking through the village, he was boasting, "I am the greatest chief there is! I am the greatest chief there is!" An old woman came up to the chief and said, "No, you're not. I know a chief who is greater than you."

The great chief reeled back and said, "What! Who is this great chief?! There is no chief greater than I am!"

The old woman said, "Um, well, if you come to my house tomorrow at noon, I will introduce you to this great chief."

The chief said, "Very well, old woman, grandmother, I will be there tomorrow at noon and we will see who is the greater chief."

The chief went home and slept very soundly, in order to gain strength and beauty during the night. In the morning, he did his work around the house, put on his finest clothing, his eagle and hawk feathers, medicine bundles, necklaces, and beads. When he was finished, he knew that, if it was to be a fight of strength, he would win, and, if it was to be a fight of beauty, he would win. He went to the old woman's home and called, "Old woman, grandmother, I am here, it is noon."

"Come in, come in."

The great chief walks in, sees the old woman, sitting against the wall, and sees a baby crawling around on the floor. "Where is the great chieftain of whom you spoke, has he or she not arrived yet?"

The old woman motions to the baby and says, "Oh, this is the great chief."

The chief yells angrily, "What do you mean, are you trying to play a trick on me, this is just a baby!"

The baby, frightened by the sudden, loud, angry voice, begins to cry. The chief is flustered by the crying, pulls his eagle and hawk feathers from his hair, and brushes the baby's cheeks with them. He pulls off his medicine bundles and holds them under the baby's nose. He pulls off the necklaces and beads and jingles them in the baby's ears. The baby, listening to the necklaces, smelling the bundles, and feeling the feathers, very quietly stops crying.

The old woman says, "You see, even you, 'the Great Chief', had to stop talking to take care of the needs of the baby. The baby won the fight, the baby won the battle. In any hut, in any home, the baby is always the greatest chief, for everyone loves and obeys implicitly whatever that baby asks. In any hut, in any home, the baby is the greatest chief."

The chief responds, "Yes, you are right, old woman, grandmother. You and the great baby chief have taught me a great lesson. I accept what your words have taught me." The chief began to put the necklaces and bundles around his neck, the eagle and hawk feathers back into his hair, and was just turning to leave. At this moment, the baby said, "Goo - goo!" This was the baby's victory cry, and ever since then, babies all over the world say, "Goo - goo." Thanks to this story, we know what that means. The baby is saying, "I am the world's greatest chief -- Goo - Goo!"

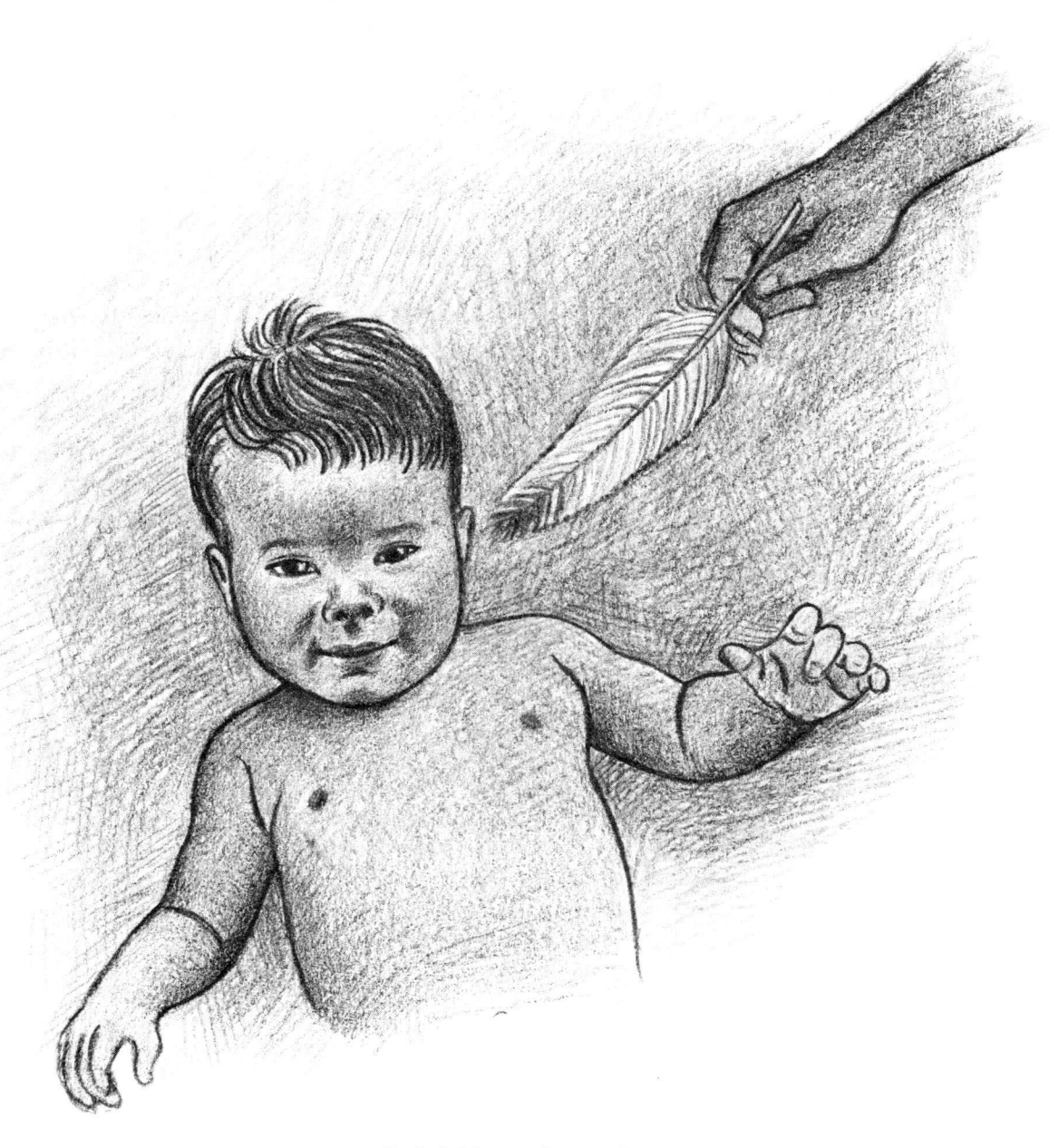

"Tickling the Baby"
-- Nina Uccello

THE DOVE AND THE HAWK by Fritz Eichenberg

Affirmation

-- Nancy Schimmel

I am the peace movement

I am growing faster than corn in Kansas

Faster than the computer industry

Faster than the national debt

And I am hungry

I chew up bullets and spit out nails

I chew up tanks and spit out playgrounds

I chew up bombers and spit out bridges

I can rock a baby with one hand and throttle a
   missile appropriation with the other and never
   miss a beat

I can walk around the world in a day and shake hands
   with a million people and come home singing

I am big and getting bigger

I am loud and getting louder

And nothing can stop me

* About the Contributors *

Floating Eaglefeather is a travelling storyteller who gathers and tells stories from around the world, underlining the unity of life by his choice of stories. He was a board member of the American Storytelling Resource Center, California, and executive secretary of Renaissance Artists and Writers Association, No. America. He has performed in many parts of the world, from the Peace Museum in Hiroshima to the one in Chicago. This has given him an opportunity to meet many children of all ages -- from toddler to staff-carrier. He has written a book of poetry, The Kiss of God, and edited a book of stories and poems, As One Is, So One Sees. A Maya mestizo of Honduras, C.A. by birth, he now considers himself a world citizen.

Ernest Sternglass, Ph.D. is Emeritus Professor of Radiology, specializing in Radiological Physics, at the University of Pittsburgh Medical School, as well as past president of the Pittsburgh Chapter of the Federation of American Scientists, a Fellow of the American Physical Society, a member of the Radiological Society of North America and the American Association of Physics in Medicine. He has testified on low-level radiation before the Joint Committee on Atomic Energy and many other groups across the globe. He has written two books on radiation's effects on humans -- Low-Level Radiation, and Secret Fallout: Low-Level Radiation from Hiroshima to Three-Mile Island.

Peggy Lipschutz is a painter, illustrator, and cartoonist from Evanston, Illinois. Her works include illustrations for The Ella Jenkins Songbook for Children, and the two-volume autobiography of veteran labor journalist, Art Shields, and she is also the art editor of the national rank-and-file labor journal, Labor Today. Her specialty is "chalk-talks" -- visual and verbal cartooning presenting serious topics with speed and humor. She has presented these chalk-talks from coast to coast, both live and on TV, concentrating on health, justice, and, above all, peace.

Rebecca Armstrong is a calligrapher of life. Her relaxed discipline is to be seen in the lines and curves of her calligraphy, but also in her voice and music when she tells stories or sings alone, with sister Jenny, or with her parents, Scottish/Irish tale-tellers and musicians, Gerry and George Armstrong. With her choice of songs, she can give joy and escape, but can also alert to and comfort from the fears of war. She and Peggy perform together in "Songs You Can See", in which Becky sings while Peggy draws. Together, they have captivated countless audiences.